Oxford School *Shakespeare*

A Midsummer Night's Dream

edited by
Roma Gill, OBE
M.A. *Cantab.*, B. Litt. *Oxon*

OXFORD

OXFORD
UNIVERSITY PRESS

Great Clarendon Street, Oxford OX2 6DP

Oxford University Press is a department of the University of Oxford.
It furthers the University's objective of excellence in research,
scholarship, and education by publishing worldwide in

Oxford   New York

Auckland   Cape Town   Dar es Salaam   Hong Kong   Karachi
Kuala Lumpur   Madrid   Melbourne   Mexico City   Nairobi
New Delhi   Shanghai   Taipei   Toronto

With offices in

Argentina   Austria   Brazil   Chile   Czech Republic   France   Greece
Guatemala   Hungary   Italy   Japan   Poland   Portugal   Singapore
South Korea   Switzerland   Thailand   Turkey   Ukraine   Vietnam

Oxford is a registered trade mark of Oxford University Press
in the UK and in certain other countries

First published 1997
Reprinted in this new edition 2005

British Library Cataloguing in Publication Data

Data available

ISBN-13: 978 0 19 832150 7

12

Printed and bound by Creative Print and Design Wales, Ebbw Vale

The Publisher would like to thank the
following for permission to reproduce
photographs:

p.x Donald Cooper/Photostage; p.xiv Donald
Cooper/Photostage; p.xvii Donald
Cooper/Photostage; p.xxii Donald
Cooper/Photostage; p.18 Donald
Cooper/Photostage; p.32 Donald
Cooper/Photostage; p.36 The Globe Theatre;
p.58 Donald Cooper/Photostage; p.74
Donald Cooper/Photostage; p.84 Donald
Cooper/Photostage; p.88 Shakespeare's
Globe; p.129 Corbis UK Ltd.

Cover image by Ronald Grant Archive.

Artwork is by Shirley Tourret and David
Cusik.

Oxford School Shakespeare
edited by Roma Gill
with additional material by Judith Kneen

Macbeth
Much Ado About Nothing
Henry V
Romeo and Juliet
A Midsummer Night's Dream
Twelfth Night
Hamlet
The Merchant of Venice
Othello
Julius Caesar
The Tempest
The Taming of the Shrew
King Lear
As You Like It
Antony and Cleopatra
Measure for Measure
Henry IV Part I
The Winter's Tale
Coriolanus
Love's Labour's Lost
Richard II

Contents

Introduction

About the Play

A civilised society

The play begins and ends in Athens. Here is Duke Theseus's palace, and the home of Peter Quince the joiner. It is a civilized society in which every man knows his place, from the Duke (whose function it is to administer law and justice) to the humblest workman (who must take care not to offend the ladies). This is where we first meet the human characters: Theseus and Hippolyta are eagerly awaiting their wedding-day; the four young lovers have already got their relationships in a tangle; and the workmen have begun to plan a project far more adventurous than anything they have undertaken before.

Into the forest

Theseus and Hippolyta remain in Athens whilst we (as audience or readers) accompany the lovers and the workmen on their separate expeditions outside the city walls and into the forest that surrounds Athens. The forest belongs to the fairies, and Athenian law does not operate here: Oberon, the fairy king, tries to impose some kind of rule, but he is not a god and he makes mistakes. The first scene in the forest shows us the fairies at their best and at their worst. At their best they are caring for the wild flowers: at their worst they are quarrelling furiously, and their quarrels have serious repercussions in the lives of human beings.

Midsummer madness

The lovers and the workmen enter the fairy realm and soon become aware of the strangeness of their surroundings. It is a strangeness that grows more frightening as night approaches, and although most of the workmen manage to escape (with some damage to their clothing), the lovers become more deeply embroiled in their own problems until, quite exhausted, they lie down to sleep, feeling alone and afraid.

The time spent in the forest is the period immediately before Theseus's wedding, which has been arranged so that

> the moon, like to a silver bow
> New bent in heaven, shall behold the night

Of our solemnities.   (1, 1, 9–11)

Before a new moon is seen, the only night light comes from the stars—and even these are 'overcast' when Oberon orders Puck to mislead the quarrelling lovers (*Act 3*, Scene 2).

But although the night is dark, it is very short—the shortest night of the year. In England, and in most European countries, the night before midsummer day has always been associated with magic, fairies, and lovers. It is also a time for madness, and the phrase 'midsummer madness' is still used to describe a state of mind which is abnormal (perhaps affected by the heat of the sun—or by fairy power) but which does not last long.

A return to order

Light dawns when Theseus and Hippolyta come out of the city in order to pay some kind of homage to the midsummer season. Slowly the lovers recover from their temporary 'madness'—and we all return to Athens and civilization, where the play ends with three weddings— a triple celebration of this civilization. Without an ordered society, marriage is impossible; and every wedding—every permanent bond between two people—strengthens the society in which it occurs.

Finally it is the turn of the fairies to enter 'foreign' territory: they come from the wood to the palace in order to bless the three marriages within the play—and perhaps another marriage, which Queen Elizabeth herself attended and which may well have been celebrated by a performance of Shakespeare's play. The bride, Elizabeth Carey, was the Queen's god-daughter, and both her father and her grandfather (Lord Hunsdon, the Lord Chamberlain) were patrons of the company of actors to which Shakespeare belonged, and for which he wrote his plays.

A popular favourite

The play has always been popular with audiences. It was a favourite in the nineteenth century, when it was performed in London with real rabbits, and there have been many open-air productions in the twentieth century, as well as a very imaginative American film; parts of the plot have been used for ballet and opera, and it has inspired painters and musicians. Mendelssohn's 'Wedding March', first written in the early nineteenth century to introduce Act 5, is still the most popular music played at English weddings when the newly-married couple walk out of the church together.

Leading Characters in the Play

In *A Midsummer Night's Dream* there are four story-lines, and four sets of characters:

1 The Royals:
Theseus
Hippolyta

These two are originally figures from Greek mythology. There are many narratives which tell how Theseus, a legendary ruler of Athens, fought with various monsters and killed the Minotaur that threatened to destroy the island of Crete; how princesses fell in love with him; and how he defeated an invasion of Amazons, and married their Queen, Hippolyta.

The Amazons were a nation of women-warriors, who despised men and refused to marry them. It was thought that they came originally from Africa, and that they conquered almost the whole of Asia before they were defeated by Theseus. Theseus and Hippolyta take little part in the action of the play, but their marriage provides a framework and an occasion for the stories of the other characters.

2 The Lovers:
Hermia and
Lysander
Helena and
Demetrius

These are creatures of Shakespeare's imagination, although he took their names from the classical traditions that gave him the persons of Theseus and Hippolyta, and an idea for their story from one of Chaucer's *Canterbury Tales*. Because the lovers are Athenians from ancient Greece, they worship the gods of Greek mythology: Hermia is prepared to become a nun in the service of Diana, goddess of chastity, and Helena blames Cupid, the mischievous god of love, for all her misfortunes.

But these lovers are not figures from the dim and distant past. Hermia is a hot-tempered young woman who is very conscious of the fact that she is smaller than Helena, and rather jealous of her friend's fair-haired beauty—whilst the tall, blonde Helena suffers agonies of unrequited love for the man (Demetrius) who once promised to marry her and who has now fallen in love with Hermia.

3 The Workmen:

Often, when these comedy characters are mentioned in the play, the audience is reminded that they too are Greek—'Hard-handed men that work in Athens here' (5, 1, 72). But we ignore the reminder. The amateur actors behave like sixteenth-century Englishmen. When these characters wish to express themselves emphatically, or to utter a mild oath, they do not call upon the classical gods. Instead they swear 'By'r lakin' or 'Marry'—invoking the Christian Virgin Mary.

Their names declare their occupations.

Quince   the carpenter; his name is taken from the 'quoins'—wedge-shaped pieces of wood used in building.

Bottom   the weaver, so called because in weaving the thread is wound on a reel or 'bottom'.

Flute   the bellows-mender; a whistling sound is produced when bellows are squeezed to blow air either on to coals (to make the fire burn) or into church organ-pipes.

Snout   the tinker, who repaired the 'snouts'—spouts—of kettles.

Starveling   the tailor, who owes his name to the popular belief that tailors were always very thin.

Snug   the joiner, who must make the pieces of wood fit snugly together.

Although they are called 'rude mechanicals' (3, 2, 9), it must not be assumed that these workmen have had no education. Snug, obviously, was not very bright at his lessons, and he confesses that he is 'slow of study' (1, 2, 59). But Elizabethan tradesmen certainly sent their sons to school, and this is perhaps where Bottom learned the long words that he is so proud to use (although he is not very sure of their meanings). Peter Quince is the most intelligent of the workmen: he can correct mispronunciations and misunderstandings, and he knows about the fables of classical mythology—part of the national curriculum of the grammar school.

4 The Fairies: Every community has its own superstitions concerning beings that are neither human (although they may appear in human form) nor divine. These are immortal, and usually ageless. They possess some magical powers, and they can use these either to assist mortals or to annoy them. The beliefs vary from one nation to another, from one county to another—and sometimes one small village cannot agree with its nearest neighbour about the invisible creatures that live in the nearby woods, or underneath the hill, or at the bottom of the garden. Modern technology has made the whole world one 'global village'— and just what creatures inhabit cyberspace?

Titania is the fairy with the longest history. The Roman poet Ovid gives this name to Diana, goddess of chastity, and although Shakespeare's fairy queen is certainly not a goddess, there are some similarities between Titania and the pagan deities. Early in the play Titania speaks (2, 1, 123–37) of having women followers (like an order of nuns) who devote themselves to her service. Most importantly, she is convinced that her quarrels with Oberon have caused havoc in the lives of the 'human mortals': the fairies have neglected the proper ceremonials, and as a result the elements—wind, rain, and sun—have been disturbed (2, 1, 81–117). Titania is, however, quite unlike the classical goddess of chastity, because she is married to Oberon.

Oberon Titania's husband first appears as king of the fairies in a French romance written in the fifteenth century and translated into English shortly before Shakespeare wrote his play.

Shakespeare gives Oberon a wife, and he also suggests that, like Titania, Oberon belongs to the period of classical myth. Titania accuses Oberon of being in love with Hippolyta; and Oberon in turn accuses his wife of giving too much assistance to Theseus (2, 1, 76–80). There is no 'truth' in these mutual accusations, of course; as Titania says, they are 'the forgeries of jealousy' (2, 1, 81).

In the play, however, these 'forgeries' serve two useful purposes. It is common for husbands and wives to taunt each other about past love affairs, and this quarrel makes Oberon and Titania seem much more real. Also, because we recognize Hippolyta and Theseus as full-sized human beings, we are encouraged to think of the fairy king and queen in the same dimensions. Shakespeare does *not* want us to do this with the other fairies who are their attendants and courtiers.

Peaseblossom
Cobweb
Moth
Mustardseed Only four of the fairy attendants have names, but as we read we imagine that there are many more than four of these tiny creatures. Certainly one nameless fairy has a 'speaking part', and it is he (or perhaps she) who first describes fairy forms and activities. We are told (in *Act 2, Scene 1*) that the fairies are very small: compared to them cowslips are 'tall', and acorn-cups make safe hiding-places. The four names suggest that their owners are not only tiny but also very fragile: a cobweb is easily brushed aside, and moths must be handled very delicately.

Shakespeare had no source for these fairies except his own invention. English children today recognize them easily, but they were quite unknown before *A Midsummer Night's Dream* was written. When narratives composed earlier than this play tell of 'fairies' they refer to quite different creatures who are the size of human beings and usually hostile to mortals. A particularly unpleasant trait of these 'old style' fairies was their habit of stealing beautiful human children from their cradles, and substituting weak or ugly fairy children—'changelings'.

Shakespeare's fairies, however, care about human beings. They also (we are told) look after the wild flowers in the woods. But their chief occupation is dancing, usually in a formal circle, and it seems as though this activity casts some kind of spell, making the place safe and even holy. Oberon explains carefully that he and the fairies of his court are not evil spirits, like the ghosts of damned souls who can only appear during the hours of darkness (3, 2, 388–93). Yet the fairies are particularly associated with night, and they are most awake when mortals are asleep.

Puck Probably the most famous of all Shakespeare's fairy characters is Puck—but Puck is not the product of the dramatist's own imagination. Until Shakespeare wrote *A Midsummer Night's Dream* it was possible to speak of *a* puck, or *the* puck. A puck was simply a *kind* of fairy, and stories about pucks are common throughout the British Isles. They were mischievous beings, able to change their shapes into human or animal forms, and especially likely to appear as flickering lights to mislead travellers in the night. At heart, however, the puck was a friendly spirit—and sometimes called 'Robin Goodfellow': he was sympathetic to the mortals who spoke politely to him; kind to lovers; and always ready to help the housewife who tried to keep her home clean and tidy. Shakespeare refers to many of the qualities that tradition attributes to the puck, and he places this fairy at the centre of his play. Puck is given an official position in the fairy court, where his job is to 'jest to Oberon, and make him smile' (2, 1, 44). He is Oberon's agent when the king of the fairies tries to help the human lovers; and it is he who is responsible for all the complications that arise in the play.

Perhaps it is also Puck who expresses the feelings of the audience when he contemplates the situation and remarks, with gentle amusement, 'Lord what fools these mortals be' (3, 2, 115).

Synopsis

Act 1

SCENE 1   Theseus passes judgement on Hermia, who refuses to marry Demetrius and agrees to run away with Lysander. They confide in Helena, who is already in love with Demetrius.

SCENE 2   Some Athenian workmen plan to produce a play for the wedding-day of Duke Theseus.

Act 2

SCENE 1   Oberon and Titania are quarrelling, but the fairy king sends Puck to fetch a magic flower—which will also help Helena to secure the love of Demetrius.

SCENE 2   Oberon sprinkles magic juice on Titania's eyes; Puck mistakes Lysander for Demetrius, and anoints his eyes so that he falls in love with Helena. Hermia is left alone in the forest.

Act 3

SCENE 1   The workmen meet in the forest but Puck interrupts their rehearsal, puts a false head on Bottom, and leads him to Titania—who falls in love with him.

SCENE 2   Oberon discovers Puck's mistake and tries to correct it by sprinkling the juice on Demetrius's eyes. Now Helena thinks she is being mocked by Hermia and the two men. Oberon orders Puck to keep the rivals apart until the situation can be remedied.

Act 4

SCENE 1   Bottom teases the fairies until he falls asleep. Oberon takes the spell off Titania's eyes, and all the fairies depart, leaving the lovers to be woken up by Theseus. Finally Bottom wakes up.

SCENE 2   Bottom returns to Athens, and the workmen prepare to go to the palace.

Act 5

SCENE 1   After their wedding Theseus and Hippolyta, with the other four lovers, watch the performance of 'Pyramus and Thisbe' before going to bed. When the mortals have retired, the fairies return to bless the marriages.

A Midsummer Night's Dream: Commentary

ACT 1

SCENE 1   Only four days now ... Theseus can't wait for his wedding-day, but his intended bride Hippolyta tries to soothe his impatience (which she appears not to share) with the promise that everything will happen in due course. And there will be all the proper pomp and ceremony for this great occasion in the civilized and law-abiding Athenian court.

But suddenly the gracious calm is broken by an angry father. Egeus drags his rebellious daughter Hermia before the highest authority in the land in a desperate attempt to force her to marry Demetrius, the man of *his* choice. The rhythms of the verse alter, allowing Egeus to splutter out his indignation whilst Theseus attempts to talk sense to a sullen and resolute Hermia. She must choose between Demetrius and death, and not even Theseus can deny the 'ancient privilege of Athens' that allows Egeus to make such demands on his child. But he is able to offer another option: Hermia could become a nun!

Undaunted, Hermia persists in her loyalty to Lysander the man she really loves. Theseus—perhaps playing for time—gives her four days to change her mind. Her decision must be made on his wedding-day.

Theseus, clearly, is sympathetic to Hermia's cause—and his sympathy influences the feelings of the audience. With great tact he draws Egeus and Demetrius away with him, leaving the two lovers alone on stage. They lament their woes in verse that draws attention to itself *as* verse—poetic and unrealistic:

> **Lysander**
> The course of true love never did run smooth;
> But either it was different in blood—
> > **Hermia**
> > O cross! too high to be enthrall'd to low.
> **Lysander**
> Or else misgraffed in respect of years—
> > **Hermia**
> > O spite! too old to be engag'd to young.

It is a skilful technique. Hermia's situation could be very serious—a matter of life or death—and Shakespeare wants the audience to sympathize with the dilemma. But he does not want to make them over-anxious and this artificial, 'patterned' verse serves to remind us that this is a play—a comedy—and no one is seriously in danger. We can wonder how things will work out; but we can be sure that the ending will be a happy one.

After we have heard Lysander's plot to escape from Athens, we meet the last member of the set of lovers. We already know that Helena is desperately in love with Demetrius, and an audience should be able to see that in every way, Helena is the opposite of Hermia: she is tall and fair where Hermia is small and dark, and whilst Hermia is quick, hot-tempered, and energetic, Helena is slow to anger and languid. Now she seems almost to be *enjoying* her misery in her lyrical rhyming verse, and she has no hesitation in betraying Hermia's confidence: she will tell Demetrius of the lovers' flight into the forest, Demetrius will be sure to follow Hermia, and then Helena (expecting more humiliation from the man she loves) will chase after Demetrius.

SCENE 2   The next scene is in complete contrast: passionate emotions and artificial, patterned verse give place to everyday concerns and easy, colloquial prose—although there is conflict here too, in the power struggle between Peter Quince and Nick Bottom.

A group of workmen are intending to put on a play to celebrate the Duke's wedding. As Quince introduces his actors, calling them 'man by man, according to the scrip' and naming their occupations, it is clear that these are *English* workmen, from Shakespeare's own Elizabethan period. The play they have chosen to perform is based on a sophisticated story from Greek mythology—and it is hopelessly unsuited to their talents and understanding.

Although some of the company are hesitant, Bottom the weaver is confident that he could play every single part himself. Quince needs all his tact and diplomacy to persuade him that he can play no part but Pyramus ('a most lovely, gentlemanlike man'). Once this is settled it only remains to fix the time and place for the first rehearsal: 'tomorrow night . . . in the palace wood . . . by moonlight'.

ACT 2

SCENE 1   In another complete change of mood and scene, the audience arrives in the forest before the lovers and the amateur actors have time to escape from Athens. Here all is fairyland and prettiness—at least to begin with, as Puck and the anonymous Fairy establish the scale of things by describing their activities. But soon we hear of yet another conflict.

There is a child at the centre of this quarrel. Titania and Oberon, being spirits, can have no children. Titania has adopted a little orphan boy—but Oberon wants the child to become one of *his* followers. The fairy king and queen have been quarrelling for a long time over this very human business, and the quarrels of supernatural beings bring supernatural disasters. The seasons of the year have got mixed up: harvests are ruined by tempests, and roses are blooming in winter; the climate is wet and cold, and 'rheumatic diseases do abound'. The human beings are suffering, but although Titania is sorry for them, neither she nor Oberon will relent.

Oberon, however, has a scheme for getting his own way. In one of the play's most beautiful passages he describes the magical powers of a certain herb, 'love-in-idleness', which had once been hit by one of Cupid's arrows and consequently acquired that arrow's potency. Oberon plans to use this charm to distract Titania and aquire the boy—but the flower's uses do not stop there.

Drawing a black cloak around him ('I am invisible'), Oberon listens to the arguments as Demetrius tries to shake off the adoring Helena, who has followed him to the woods as he pursues the runaway lovers. She is undeterred by his threats of violence and the danger of the solitary wilderness—and invites him to do his worst:

> I am your spaniel; and, Demetrius,
> The more you beat me I will fawn on you.
> Use me but as your spaniel: spurn me, strike me . . .

The unseen Oberon decides to protect Helena and change Demetrius' mind—but when he gives instructions to Puck ('Thou shalt know the man By the Athenian garments he hath on'), the audience can guess what will happen next.

SCENE 2   Titania dismisses her attendants, and sleeps. For 'the third part of a minute' she is at Oberon's mercy. Quickly he sprinkles the flower-juice on her eyelids, with a magic spell. Titania sleeps on, invisible to other characters now appearing on the stage.

Lysander and Hermia are tired and lost—but in complete harmony with each other, speaking in easy rhyming couplets and taking delight in the innocent double meanings that their loving language produces. Soon they too are asleep, keeping the modest distance which Hermia thinks suitable for 'a virtuous bachelor and a maid'. But that space between them is enough to convince Puck that he has found the 'lack-love' described by Oberon. Again the magic juice is sprinkled—and now Demetrius and Helena run across the stage . . .

Helena is exhausted, but still has breath to lament her situation—and increase the delightful suspense of the audience—before she notices the sleeping Lysander:

But who is here?—Lysander, on the ground?
Dead, or asleep? I see no blood, no wound.
Lysander, if you live, good sir, awake!

Lysander's reaction is instantaneous—

And run through fire I will for thy sweet sake!

His exaggerated declarations of love seem like cruel mockery to Helena. She runs away from him, leaving Lysander to turn on the sleeping Hermia with a violent hatred that must somehow be reflected in her dreams. When she wakes, she finds herself quite alone, abandoned in a dreadful wood.

SCENE 1   ACT 3

As Hermia wanders away into the forest, the workmen assemble for their first rehearsal. Staging the play in the great hall of the palace will present some practical problems—but Bottom is endlessly resourceful: moonshine can come through the chamber window, 'Lion' can show his face through his mask, and 'Wall' can make himself known by 'some lime, or some rough-cast about him'. These actors have both too much, and too little, imagination; and they assume that their audience will think as they do.

But they have an unseen audience now, and one who is ready to play his part in the action. Whilst Flute is struggling with Thisbe's lines, Puck transforms Bottom into a monster by placing an ass's head upon his shoulders. The rehearsal is abandoned and Bottom, deserted by his terrified comrades, tries to keep up his courage with a song. That wakes Titania from her 'flowery bed'. Under the influence of Oberon's herbal drug she falls instantly in love with Bottom.

Bottom, unchanged despite his metamorphosis, is fully in control of the situation. He is smugly self-satisfied with his ability to command the fairy attendants, and he accepts Titania's pretty declaration of love and admiration with only a little embarrassment—

> Methinks, mistress, you should have little reason for that. And yet, to say the truth, reason and love keep little company together nowadays.

The joke has rather more meaning than he intended!

SCENE 2   Just as Puck is reporting the success of his mission, Demetrius and Hermia burst on to the stage. Hermia, driven 'past the bounds Of maiden's patience', accuses Demetrius of murdering Lysander—and Oberon realizes that Puck has 'mistaken quite And laid the love juice on some true love's sight'. He tries to remedy the mistake whilst Demetrius, exhausted with argument, lies down to sleep; but he only adds to the confusion. When Demetrius awakes he catches sight of Helena—and immediately declares his passion for her—in verse that is comically bad:

> O Helen, goddess, nymph, perfect, divine!
> To what, my love, shall I compare thine eyne?
> Crystal is muddy! O, how ripe in show
> Thy lips, those kissing cherries, tempting grow.

Helena, already pursued by an amorous Lysander, is completely bewildered and sees all this as some kind of conspiracy—in which Hermia must also have a part.

The comedy, in rhyming couplets, continues for a short time, but the verse loses its rhyme when the two girls join battle with each other. At first Helena laments the lost innocence of the schooldays they shared together, but soon (when Hermia will not share in this nostalgia) she remembers a quite different picture:

> when she is angry she is keen and shrewd;
> She was a vixen when she went to school.

The fight between the 'painted maypole' (Helena) and the 'puppet' (Hermia) soon involves their lovers, who threaten real, physical violence and depart to find a suitable duelling-ground—followed quickly by Helena, whose boasted longer legs will take her easily out of Hermia's reach.

Oberon's magic, and Puck's organizational skills, are necessary to restore harmony. Once again the verse switches to spell-binding rhyme: dawn is approaching, and the things of night—ghosts, evil spirits, darkness, and misunderstanding—must retreat before the daylight. First, however, the lovers must blunder their ways through the darkness of Puck's 'drooping fog', following deceptive voices until they drop with fatigue—all in the same place—and the delighted spirit can restore their proper vision.

ACT 4

SCENE 1

As the spell-bound lovers sleep, Titania brings Bottom to the forefront of the action, where he revels in the attentions of his new servants (although they cannot understand what he wants) until he is overtaken by 'an exposition of sleep'.

Oberon contemplates the grotesque combination of fairy queen and ass-headed mortal weaver, and is overcome with a kind of pity. Titania has already relented, and released her hold on the little Indian boy. When her sight is restored with Oberon's spell-remover she shudders at the monster beside her. Puck removes Bottom's false head, and then

Oberon and Titania, with their fairy attendants, perform a magic dance before vanishing away into the light of day—which is brought in by Theseus and his hunting party.

After some boasting about his hounds, Theseus's eye alights on the sleeping lovers who are confused and embarrassed in the presence of the Duke of Athens. Worse, Hermia's father is with him. Theseus is amused, but Egeus is furious—although Demetrius tries to wriggle out of the situation by excusing his love for Hermia as a passing fancy, the whim of a sick man which passes with his return to health.

The lovers follow the hunters back into Athens, wondering about the events of the night but unable to remember with any clarity. Lastly Bottom comes to his senses, and struggles to recall his 'most rare vision'.

SCENE 2   In this short scene (which covers the passage of time between the awakening in the forest and the wedding celebrations of the following day) the workmen lament the loss of Bottom—but their grief is short-lived. With characteristic bounce and efficiency ('good strings to your beards, new ribbons to your pumps'), Bottom hurries them off to the palace.

ACT 5

SCENE 1   The formalities of marriage are all completed, and now there is time for some little discussion of the events of the previous night—which Theseus is inclined to dismiss as the fantastic imaginings of brain-sick lovers, 'more strange than true'. But supper has been eaten and there are still some hours before bedtime which must be filled with some kind of merriment. Theseus is attracted to the workmen's play of 'Pyramus and Thisbe', which his programme describes as 'A tedious brief scene' offering 'very tragical mirth'. The pompous master-of-ceremonies sneers at the play and despises the actors 'Which never labour'd in their minds till now', but Theseus is a generous ruler, and understands that the play is being offered in 'simpleness and duty' and must be graciously accepted.

We realize what a great occasion this is for the 'rude mechanicals' when Quince stutters his way through a formal address to the audience, but his fluency increases when he speaks the Prologue—a conventional device used in early Elizabethan plays to help the audience (who might not always get a good view of the stage) to follow the play. The problems that were raised before the forest rehearsal have all been solved now—although the solutions provide almost as much entertainment as the play itself and its enthusiastic actors.

Lysander and Demetrius compete with each other in wisecracking throughout the performance, and however much Theseus tries at first to restrain them, he is forced to share their laughter after Bottom's protracted death scene and Flute's nonsensical lamentations over the body of 'Pyramus'. The play has served its function, however, and 'well beguil'd The heavy gait of night'. Theseus dismisses his guests to their marriage-beds, and leaves the stage to the fairies and the hypnotic rhymes and rhythms of their final blessing.

'Of Imagination all Compact'

The magic—one kind of magic—ends when Oberon and Titania leave the stage. Puck, with his broom and epilogue, introduces a down-to-earth note when he speaks directly to the audience, suggesting that they too, like the lovers and Bottom, have been asleep—'you have but slumber'd here'. All the strange goings-on that they have witnessed have been 'No more yielding but a dream'. He speaks of 'shadows', and at first it seems that he is referring to the other fairies—but in fact Puck is speaking on behalf of all the actors who have taken part in *A Midsummer Night's Dream*.

Shadows of the stage
In his other plays, Shakespeare often calls actors 'shadows', and in *Act 5* of this play we can almost hear Shakespeare speaking through Theseus when the Duke, excusing the amateur actors of 'Pyramus and Thisbe', explains that

> The best in this kind are but shadows, and the worst are no worse, if imagination amend them.

Shakespeare believed that actors have no substance or identity *in themselves*. They exist in order to lend their bodies and their talents to the personalities that the dramatist has created, and whilst the play is being performed, only these characters—Theseus, Titania, Bottom, Hermia, and the rest—are important.

A leap of imagination
The spectators have agreed—by coming to watch the performance—to share in the dramatist's imagination, and to bring along *their own* imaginations to supply anything that is lacking in the production. So when Oberon says 'Ill met by moonlight, proud Titania', the audience must be prepared to believe that it is night, and the moon is shining in the woodlands outside Athens—even though the performance is taking place in broad daylight, and in the middle of London.

This dramatic imagination is something that the workmen cannot comprehend:

> **Quince**
> But there is two hard things: that is, to bring the moonlight into a chamber; for, you know, Pyramus and Thisbe meet by moonlight.

Snug
Doth the moon shine that night we play our play?
Bottom
A calendar, a calendar! Look in the almanac; find out
moonshine, find out moonshine.

The more they strive for actual reality, and the more attributes that Wall
carries around with him (5, 1, 159), the further they get from the realism
they hope to achieve. Theseus quite rightly says that imagination will
improve—'amend'—the mechanicals' performance; but Hippolyta
shows a true understanding of the situation when she points out that 'It
must be your imagination then, and not theirs'.

Shaping fantasies

At the beginning of *Act 5*, Theseus explains how the poet's imagination works—surely Shakespeare's own account of his own 'shaping
fantasies'. The poet is 'of imagination all compact', and his imagination 'bodies forth The forms of things unknown'. Perfect examples of
this are the tiny fairies, Peaseblossom, Cobweb, Moth, and
Mustardseed, who were totally unknown until Shakespeare wrote this
play, and his pen 'Turn[ed] them to shapes' and gave 'airy nothing A
local habitation and a name'.

Theseus tells us that the poet is first of all an observer, and that
his eyes survey the whole of his universe—'from heaven to earth,
from earth to heaven'. This gives him his material: most of the time he
does not invent from nothing. In the play we can see how Shakespeare
has read classical mythology, and French fiction; how he is well-
informed about folk-lore, and understands the life of the countryside;
and how he has watched the workmen of his own town and time.
Reading and observation gave him the raw materials, and then the
power of Shakespeare's unique imagination (aided by the craftsman-
ship of the experienced dramatist and poet) performed a miracle.
And this is called
A Midsummer Night's Dream.

Shakespeare's Verse

Blank verse

Shakespeare's plays are mainly written in 'blank verse', the form preferred by most dramatists in the sixteenth and early seventeenth centuries. Blank verse has a regular rhythm, but does not rhyme. It is a very flexible medium, which is capable—like the human speaking voice—of a wide range of tones. Easily the best way to understand and appreciate Shakespeare's verse is to read it aloud—and don't worry if you don't understand everything! Try not to be influenced by the dominant rhythm. Instead, decide which are the most important words in each line and use the regular metre to drive them forward to the listeners. Shakespeare used a particular form of blank verse called iambic pentameter.

Iambic pentameter

In iambic pentameter the lines are ten syllables long. Each line is divided into pairs of syllables, or 'feet'. Each 'foot' has one stressed and one unstressed syllable—a pattern which often appears in normal English speech. Here is an example:

> **Theseus**
> To yóu, your fáther shóuld be ás a gód;
> One thát compós'd your béauties, yéa, and óne
> To whóm you áre but ás a fórm in wáx
> By hím imprínted, ánd withín his pówer
> To leáve the fígure, ór disfígure ít.
> Demétrius ís a wórthy géntlemán.
> **Hermia**
> So ís Lysánder.
> **Theseus**
>   Ín himsélf he ís;
> But ín this kínd, wanting your fáther's vóice,
> The óther múst be héld the wórthier.

                                          1, 1, 47–55

Here the pentameter accommodates a variety of speech tones. Theseus speaks with authority when he lectures Hermia on the proper obedience of a daughter. She passionately defends her love, and Theseus replies with calm reasonableness.

Varying stresses

In the quotation above, the lines are all regular in length, and mostly follow the normal iambic stress pattern: in each 'foot' (pair of syllables) the stress is on the second syllable. But sometimes Shakespeare deviates from the norm, writing lines that are longer or shorter than ten syllables, and varying the stress patterns for unusual emphasis: here Hermia's retort could be stressed 'So is', with the stress on the first syllable in the pair.

Dividing lines

The exchange between Theseus and Hermia shows another of Shakespeare's devices, when he divides a metrical line between two speakers:

> **Hermia**
> So is Lysander.
> **Theseus**
>   In himself he is;

This gives a sense of how quickly Theseus reacts to what Hermia has just said to him.

Dividing ideas

The same exchange shows another way in which Shakespeare varies his use of verse. Sometimes, the verse line contains the grammatical unit of meaning:

> To you, your father should be as a god;

This allows for a pause at the end of the line, before a new idea is started. At other times, the sense runs on from one line to the next:

>   within his power
> To leave the figure, or disfigure it.

This allows for the natural fluidity of speech, avoiding monotony but still maintaining the iambic rhythm.

Source, Text, and Date

In *A Midsummer Night's Dream* Shakespeare offers a glorious celebration of the powers of the human imagination. The story-line is assembled from many different sources—literature, folklore, and personal observation—but not one of these can be said to be predominant.

Shakespeare's reading for this play included 'The Knight's Tale' in Chaucer's *Canterbury Tales*, 'The Life of Theseus' in Plutarch's *Parallel Lives of the Greeks and Romans* (translated by Sir Thomas North), and Ovid's *Metamorphoses* (translated by Arthur Golding). This last seems to have been one of Shakespeare's favourite books, and he refers many times, in many of his plays, to the wondrous stories told in these poems about gods and mortals who are changed into different shapes for a variety of reasons.

It is never easy to give a precise date for Shakespeare's plays, but a complimentary reference in a list of the best contemporary English writing, Francis Meres's *Palladis Tamia*, shows that *A Midsummer Night's Dream* was known before this was registered for publication in September 1598; and the style of the play suggests that it was written in the middle of the 1590s, a very fertile period in Shakespeare's creative life.

There is some other evidence (less reliable but perhaps not entirely fanciful) that may help to fix the time of writing—most notably the Lion, the Wall, and the Wedding.

The problem with the Lion which worries the actors of 'Pyramus and Thisbe' (*Act 3*, Scene 1) might have been suggested to Shakespeare by a pamphlet published in October 1594 describing a feast in Scotland, where the scheme to bring a lion into the banqueting-hall had to be abandoned because the organizers thought that the ladies would be frightened.

The Wall that separates the lovers in 'Pyramus and Thisbe' might have been something of a real problem for Shakespeare's own company when they produced his *Romeo and Juliet*, a play whose style is very closely linked to that of *A Midsummer Night's Dream*, in around 1595.

The many compliments that seem to be directed at Queen Elizabeth I (that 'fair vestal throned by the west', 2, 1, 158) might suggest that the play was, in its present form, presented at some wedding celebration that she attended. The most likely one is that in February 1596 of her god-daughter, Elizabeth Carey, whose grandfather was Lord Hunsdon, the patron of Shakespeare's acting company, 'The Chamberlain's Men'.

The play was first published in 1600, apparently from Shakespeare's own manuscript, and this Quarto edition forms the basis of most modern texts. The present edition uses the text established by R. A. Foakes in 1984 for the New Cambridge Shakespeare.

A Midsummer Night's Dream

Characters in the Play

Theseus	*Duke of Athens*
Hippolyta	*Queen of the Amazons, betrothed to* Theseus
Egeus	*a nobleman,* Hermia's *father*
Hermia	*in love with* Lysander
Helena	*in love with* Demetrius
Lysander	
Demetrius	*young noblemen*
Philostrate	*Master of the Revels at* Theseus's *court*
Oberon	*King of the fairies*
Titania	*Queen of the fairies*
Puck	Oberon's *jester and attendant*
Peaseblossom	
Cobweb	
Moth	*Fairies attending on* Titania *and* Bottom
Mustardseed	
A Fairy	*servant of* Titania
Peter Quince	*a carpenter* (Prologue *in the play of* 'Pyramus and Thisbe')
Nick Bottom	*a weaver* (Pyramus)
Francis Flute	*a bellows-mender* (Thisbe)
Tom Snout	*a tinker* (Wall)
Robin Starveling	*a tailor* (Moonshine)
Snug	*a joiner* (Lion)

Attendants at the court of Theseus
Fairies attending on Oberon and Titania

The play begins and ends in Theseus's *palace, but most of the action takes place in the woods outside the city of Athens*

ACT 1

Act 1 Scene 1

Egeus asks Theseus to pass judgement on
Hermia, who refuses to marry Demetrius
because she loves Lysander. To escape the
father's wrath, the lovers plan to run away
together, and disclose their intentions to
Helena—who is in love with Demetrius.

1 *our nuptial hour*: the time of our
   wedding.
2 *apace*: quickly.
2–3 *four . . . moon*: there will be a full
   moon in four days' time.
4 *lingers*: makes me wait for.
5–6 *a step-dame . . . revenue*: like a
   step-mother or a widow who is growing
   old and spending a young man's
   inheritance (which he would not be
   able to claim until she died).
7 *steep*: drown.

11 *solemnities*: marriage ceremonies.

12 *youth*: young people.

15 *The pale . . . pomp*: we can't have
   miserable fellows in our festivities.

16–17 *I woo'd . . . injuries*: See 'Leading
   Characters in the play', p.vii.

18 *another key*: a different way (the
   image is from music).
19 *triumph*: public festival.

SCENE 1

Athens, the palace of Theseus: *enter* Theseus,
Hippolyta, Philostrate, *with others*

Theseus
Now, fair Hippolyta, our nuptial hour
Draws on apace; four happy days bring in
Another moon—but O, methinks, how slow
This old moon wanes! She lingers my desires,
5 Like to a step-dame or a dowager
Long withering out a young man's revenue.
Hippolyta
Four days will quickly steep themselves in night;
Four nights will quickly dream away the time;
And then the moon, like to a silver bow
10 New bent in heaven, shall behold the night
Of our solemnities.
Theseus
                        Go, Philostrate,
Stir up the Athenian youth to merriments,
Awake the pert and nimble spirit of mirth;
Turn melancholy forth to funerals;
15 The pale companion is not for our pomp.
                        [*Exit* Philostrate

Hippolyta, I woo'd thee with my sword,
And won thy love doing thee injuries;
But I will wed thee in another key,
With pomp, with triumph, and with revelling.

Enter Egeus *and his daughter* Hermia, Lysander *and* Demetrius

Egeus

20 Happy be Theseus, our renowned duke!
    Theseus
    Thanks, good Egeus. What's the news with thee?
    Egeus
    Full of vexation come I, with complaint
    Against my child, my daughter Hermia.
    Stand forth Demetrius!—My noble lord,
25 This man hath my consent to marry her.
    Stand forth, Lysander!—And, my gracious duke,
    This man hath bewitch'd the bosom of my child.
    Thou, thou, Lysander, thou hast given her rhymes,
    And interchang'd love-tokens with my child.
30 Thou hast by moonlight at her window sung
    With feigning voice verses of feigning love,
    And stolen the impression of her fantasy,
    With bracelets of thy hair, rings, gauds, conceits,
    Knacks, trifles, nosegays, sweetmeats—messengers
35 Of strong prevailment in unharden'd youth;
    With cunning hast thou filch'd my daughter's heart,
    Turn'd her obedience, which is due to me,
    To stubborn harshness. And, my gracious duke,
    Be it so she will not here, before your grace,
40 Consent to marry with Demetrius,
    I beg the ancient privilege of Athens;
    As she is mine, I may dispose of her;
    Which shall be either to this gentleman
    Or to her death, according to our law
45 Immediately provided in that case.
    Theseus
    What say you, Hermia? Be advis'd, fair maid.
    To you your father should be as a god,
    One that compos'd your beauties; yea, and one
    To whom you are but as a form in wax
50 By him imprinted, and within his power
    To leave the figure, or disfigure it.
    Demetrius is a worthy gentleman.

20 *renowned*: renownèd.

27 *bosom*: heart.
28 *rhymes*: love poetry.

31 *with feigning voice*: with a voice that pretends to be sincere.
feigning love: pretended love.
32 *stolen . . . fantasy*: caught her imagination by making an impression on her.
33 *gauds*: silly toys.
conceits: fancy things.
34 *Knacks*: knick-knacks, useless little gifts.
nosegays: bunches of flowers.
sweetmeats: sweets (chocolates would be the modern English equivalent).
35 *prevailment*: persuasive power.
unharden'd: inexperienced.
36 *filch'd*: stolen.
37 *due*: owed.
39 *Be it so*: if.
41 *I beg . . . Athens*: I claim the traditional right of an Athenian.
44–5 *law . . . case*: the law specifically designed for such cases (against which there could be no appeal).
46 *Be advis'd*: think carefully.

49–50 *but . . . imprinted*: nothing more than a wax figure that he has modelled.
51 *disfigure*: destroy.

54 *in this kind*: in a matter like this.
   wanting: lacking.
   voice: approval.
56-7 *I would . . . look*: The relationship
   (or lack of it) between seeing and
   judging, the eyes and the mind, is
   central to the concerns of the play.
56 *would*: wish.
60 *concern my modesty*: affect my
   reputation for modesty.
61 *In such a presence*: i.e. before the
   duke.
   plead my thoughts: express my
   feelings.
65 *die the death*: be legally put to death.
   abjure: renounce.
67 *question your desires*: ask yourself
   what you really want.
68 *Know . . . youth*: remember that you
   are young.
70 *livery*: habit.
71 *aye*: ever.
   mew'd: shut up.
72 *sister*: nun.
73 *moon*: Diana, goddess of the moon,
   and of chastity (see 'Leading
   Characters in the Play', p.vii).
74 *blessed*: blessèd.
   master: discipline.
   blood: passions.
75 *maiden pilgrimage*: life vowed to
   celibacy.
76 *earthlier happy*: more happy on earth.
   the rose distill'd: the rose that is
   plucked, whose scent is distilled to
   make perfume.
78 *single blessedness*: the particular
   state of grace granted (in many
   religions) to those who vow never to
   marry, and live in celibacy.
80 *virgin patent*: right to remain a virgin.
81 *his lordship*: the domination of this
   man.
   unwished: unwishèd.
   yoke: a wooden cross-piece linking
   two oxen together for the purpose of
   ploughing; from this it becomes a
   symbol of bondage and servitude.
82 *give sovereignty*: acknowledge as lord
   and master.
83 *Take . . . pause*: wait a short time
   before making your decision.
84 *sealing-day*: the day on which they will
   seal (= make official) their vows.

Hermia
So is Lysander.
   Theseus
           In himself he is;
But in this kind, wanting your father's voice,
55 The other must be held the worthier.
   Hermia
I would my father look'd but with my eyes.
   Theseus
Rather your eyes must with his judgement look.
   Hermia
I do entreat your grace to pardon me.
I know not by what power I am made bold,
60 Nor how it may concern my modesty
In such a presence here to plead my thoughts;
But I beseech your grace that I may know
The worst that may befall me in this case,
If I refuse to wed Demetrius.
   Theseus
65 Either to die the death, or to abjure
For ever the society of men.
Therefore, fair Hermia, question your desires,
Know of your youth, examine well your blood,
Whether, if you yield not to your father's choice,
70 You can endure the livery of a nun,
For aye to be in shady cloister mew'd,
To live a barren sister all your life,
Chanting faint hymns to the cold fruitless moon.
Thrice blessed they that master so their blood
75 To undergo such maiden pilgrimage;
But earthlier happy is the rose distill'd
Than that which, withering on the virgin thorn,
Grows, lives, and dies in single blessedness.
   Hermia
So will I grow, so live, so die, my lord,
80 Ere I will yield my virgin patent up
Unto his lordship, whose unwished yoke
My soul consents not to give sovereignty.
   Theseus
Take time to pause, and by the next new moon,
The sealing-day betwixt my love and me

89 *protest*: vow.
90 *aye*: ever.
    austerity: strict simplicity. In the
    Christian church nuns and monks vow
    to live in poverty, chastity, and
    obedience.
92 *crazed title*: crazèd; uncertain claim
    (because Hermia's father does not
    admit it).
94 *do . . . him*: you go and marry him.

98 *estate unto*: give to. The phrase is a
    legal one, continuing the idea that
    Hermia is a mere possession.
99 *well deriv'd*: nobly descended, of good
    family.
100 *well-possess'd*: rich in possessions.
101 *My . . . rank'd*: my financial position
    and prospects rank me as high.
    fortunes: position in life.
102 *with vantage*: even better.
104 *of*: by.
105 *prosecute my right*: persist in making
    my claim.
106 *avouch . . . head*: declare before his
    face (in his presence).
107 *Made love*: courted.
108 *soul*: affections.
109 *dotes in idolatry*: idolizes.
110 *spotted*: dishonourable.

113 *overfull of self-affairs*: too concerned
    with my own business.
114 *lose*: forget.

116 *private schooling*: advice to give you in
    private.
117 *For*: as for.
    arm: prepare.
118 *fit . . . will*: make your wishes agree
    with what your father wants.

85 For everlasting bond of fellowship,
Upon that day either prepare to die
For disobedience to your father's will,
Or else to wed Demetrius, as he would,
Or on Diana's altar to protest
90 For aye austerity and single life.
    Demetrius
Relent, sweet Hermia; and, Lysander, yield
Thy crazed title to my certain right.
    Lysander
You have her father's love, Demetrius;
Let me have Hermia's—do you marry him.
    Egeus
95 Scornful Lysander, true, he hath my love,
And what is mine my love shall render him;
And she is mine, and all my right of her
I do estate unto Demetrius.
    Lysander
I am, my lord, as well-deriv'd as he,
100 As well-possess'd: my love is more than his,
My fortunes every way as fairly rank'd,
If not with vantage, as Demetrius';
And, which is more than all these boasts can be,
I am belov'd of beauteous Hermia.
105 Why should not I then prosecute my right?
Demetrius, I'll avouch it to his head,
Made love to Nedar's daughter, Helena,
And won her soul; and she, sweet lady, dotes,
Devoutly dotes, dotes in idolatry,
110 Upon this spotted and inconstant man.
    Theseus
I must confess that I have heard so much,
And with Demetrius thought to have spoke thereof;
But, being overfull of self-affairs,
My mind did lose it. But Demetrius, come,
115 And come, Egeus. You shall go with me;
I have some private schooling for you both.
For you, fair Hermia, look you arm yourself
To fit your fancies to your father's will;
Or else the law of Athens yields you up

120 *extenuate*: mitigate, make easier.

122 *what cheer*: how are you feeling;
perhaps Hippolyta looks sad, thinking
about Hermia's difficult choice.
124 *business*: All three syllables of the
word must be pronounced.
125 *Against*: in preparation for.
125-6 *confer . . . yourselves*: discuss
something that closely concerns you.
127 *desire*: willingness.

129 *How chance*: why?

130 *Belike*: probably.
131 *Beteem*: pour down on.

132 *Ay me*: Lysander sighs.
aught: anything.

135 *blood*: social class.
135-40 *But . . . eyes*: The lovers join in a
duet of alternating lines.
136 *too high . . . low*: for a high-born lady
to be made subject to a commoner.
137 *misgraffed . . . years*: misgraffèd; ill-
matched through difference of age.

139 *stood upon*: depended on.
friends: relations.

141 *sympathy*: agreement.
142 *lay siege to*: make war on.
143 *momentany*: An old form of
'momentary'.

145 *collied*: blackened (from 'colly' = soot).

146 *spleen*: sudden passionate impulse.
unfolds: lights up.
147 *ere*: before.

149 *come to confusion*: are ruined,
destroyed.

120 (Which by no means we may extenuate)
To death, or to a vow of single life.
Come, my Hippolyta; what cheer, my love?
Demetrius and Egeus, go along;
I must employ you in some business
125 Against our nuptial, and confer with you
Of something nearly that concerns yourselves.
Egeus
With duty and desire we follow you.
[*Exeunt all but* Lysander *and* Hermia
Lysander
How now, my love? Why is your cheek so pale?
How chance the roses there do fade so fast?
Hermia
130 Belike for want of rain, which I could well
Beteem them from the tempest of my eyes.
Lysander
Ay me! For aught that I could ever read,
Could ever hear by tale or history,
The course of true love never did run smooth;
135 But either it was different in blood—
Hermia
O cross! too high to be enthrall'd to low.
Lysander
Or else misgraffed in respect of years—
Hermia
O spite! too old to be engag'd to young.
Lysander
Or else it stood upon the choice of friends—
Hermia
140 O hell, to choose love by another's eyes!
Lysander
Or, if there were a sympathy in choice,
War, death, or sickness did lay siege to it,
Making it momentany as a sound,
Swift as a shadow, short as any dream,
145 Brief as the lightning in the collied night,
That in a spleen unfolds both heaven and earth,
And, ere a man hath power to say 'Behold!',
The jaws of darkness do devour it up.
So quick bright things come to confusion.

150–1 *If then . . . destiny*: if true lovers
have always ('ever') been frustrated
('crossed'), then fate must have some
law about it.

152 *let us . . . patience*: let us learn to
endure this test with patience.

153 *Because . . . cross*: because such
frustration is quite normal.

154 *due to love*: belonging to love.

155 *fancy*: love.

156 *persuasion*: advice.

157 *dowager*: widow (see lines 5–6note).

158 *revenue*: Here (but not in line 6
above) the word must be stressed on
the second syllable.

159 *remote*: distant.
league: a rough measurement of
distance, usually about three miles.

160 *respects*: regards.

162–3 *the sharp . . . pursue us*: the harsh
Athenian law will have no power over
us.

164 *Steal forth*: creep out of.

165 *without*: outside.

167 *To do . . . May*: to perform the
(fertility) rites of May Day.

168 *stay*: wait.

169 *Cupid*: the classical god of love,
usually depicted as a blindfolded,
winged boy with a bow and two
arrows, one to inspire love, and the
other to kill love; see picture p.9.

171–8 *By . . . thee*: The rhyming couplets
confirm the sincerity of Hermia's
vows—which continue to link the
friends together throughout the scene.

171 *Venus' doves*: The classical goddess of
love often travelled in a chariot drawn
by white doves—their colour signifying
the innocence ('simplicity') of pure
love.

172 *that . . . loves*: Hermia may be
referring to the girdle worn by and
associated with Venus.

173–4 *that fire . . . seen*: Dido Queen of
Carthage flung herself on a funeral
pyre when her lover, the Trojan
Aeneas, sailed away from her; the
story is told in Virgil's *Aeneid*, Book IV.

Hermia

150 If then true lovers have been ever cross'd
It stands as an edict in destiny.
Then let us teach our trial patience,
Because it is a customary cross,
As due to love as thoughts, and dreams, and sighs,

155 Wishes, and tears—poor fancy's followers.

    Lysander

A good persuasion. Therefore hear me, Hermia:
I have a widow aunt, a dowager,
Of great revenue, and she hath no child.
From Athens is her house remote seven leagues;

160 And she respects me as her only son.
There, gentle Hermia, may I marry thee;
And to that place the sharp Athenian law
Cannot pursue us. If thou lov'st me, then
Steal forth thy father's house tomorrow night,

165 And in the wood, a league without the town
(Where I did meet thee once with Helena
To do observance to a morn of May),
There will I stay for thee.

    Hermia

                  My good Lysander,
I swear to thee by Cupid's strongest bow,

170 By his best arrow with the golden head,
By the simplicity of Venus' doves,
By that which knitteth souls and prospers loves,
And by that fire which burn'd the Carthage queen
When the false Trojan under sail was seen,

175 By all the vows that ever men have broke
(In number more than ever women spoke),
In that same place thou hast appointed me,
Tomorrow truly will I meet with thee.

    Lysander

Keep promise, love. Look, here comes Helena.

Enter Helena

Hermia

180 God speed, fair Helena! Whither away?
Helena
Call you me fair? That 'fair' again unsay.
Demetrius loves your fair: O happy fair!
Your eyes are lodestars, and your tongue's sweet air
More tuneable than lark to shepherd's ear
185 When wheat is green, when hawthorn buds appear.
Sickness is catching. O, were favour so,
Yours would I catch, fair Hermia, ere I go;
My ear should catch your voice, my eye your eye,
My tongue should catch your tongue's sweet melody.
190 Were the world mine, Demetrius being bated,
The rest I'd give to be to you translated.
O, teach me how you look, and with what art
You sway the motion of Demetrius' heart.
Hermia
I frown upon him; yet he loves me still.
Helena
195 O that your frowns would teach my smiles such skill!
Hermia
I give him curses; yet he gives me love.
Helena
O that my prayers could such affection move!
Hermia
The more I hate, the more he follows me.
Helena
The more I love, the more he hateth me.
Hermia
200 His folly, Helena, is no fault of mine.
Helena
None but your beauty; would that fault were mine!
Hermia
Take comfort: he no more shall see my face;
Lysander and myself will fly this place.
Before the time I did Lysander see,
205 Seem'd Athens as a paradise to me.
O then, what graces in my love do dwell,
That he hath turn'd a heaven unto a hell?

---

180 *God speed*: may God be with you.

182 *your fair*: your beauty.

183 *lodestars*: guiding stars.
air: sound.
184 *tuneable*: tuneful.
185 *hawthorn buds*: The hawthorn is one of the first trees to flower in the English springtime.
186 *catching*: infectious.
favour: beauty, charm.
187 *ere*: before.
190 *bated*: excepted.

191 *translated*: transferred (to become Hermia's property).

193 *sway . . . heart*: influence the way Demetrius feels.

194–201 *I frown . . . mine*: Hermia and Helena join in another formal duet (compare lines 135–40).

201 *would*: I wish.

203 *fly*: escape from.

206 *graces*: qualities.

208 *minds*: thoughts, plans.
      unfold: open, explain.
209 *Phoebe*: Another name for Diana,
      goddess of the moon.
210 *visage*: face.
      watery glass: mirror made by a stretch
      of water (a lake or pond).
211 *Decking*: trimming.
      liquid pearl: drops of dew (glistening
      like pearls); the Elizabethans thought
      that dew fell from the moon.
212 *still*: always.
213 *devis'd*: planned.
215 *faint*: delicate. The primrose is a pale
      yellow, slightly scented flower of early
      spring.
      wont: accustomed.
216 *bosoms*: hearts.
      counsel: secrets.
219 *stranger companies*: the company of
      strangers.
222 *Keep word*: keep your promise.
223 *lovers' food*: i.e. the sight of each
      other.

225 *As you . . . you*: may Demetrius love
      you as much as you love him.

226 *How . . . be!*: how happy some people
      are compared with others!
      o'er: over.

232–3 *Things . . . dignity*: The truth of this
      observation will be demonstrated in
      Act 3, when Titania falls in love with
      Bottom.
232 *holding no quantity*: having no value.
233 *transpose*: transform.
234 *mind*: imagination, intelligence.
236 *Nor. . . taste*: and love's intelligence
      has no judgement.
237 *figure*: represent.
      unheedy: thoughtless.
239 *beguil'd*: deceived.
240 *waggish*: playful.
      in game: in fun.
      themselves forswear: break promises.
241 *the boy . . . everywhere*: love, like a
      little boy, breaks his promises
      everywhere.

Lysander
Helen, to you our minds we will unfold:
Tomorrow night, when Phoebe doth behold
210 Her silver visage in the watery glass,
Decking with liquid pearl the bladed grass
(A time that lovers' flights doth still conceal),
Through Athens' gates we have devis'd to steal.
Hermia
And in the wood, where often you and I
215 Upon faint primrose beds were wont to lie,
Emptying our bosoms of their counsel sweet,
There my Lysander and myself shall meet,
And thence from Athens turn away our eyes
To seek new friends and stranger companies.
220 Farewell, sweet playfellow; pray thou for us,
And good luck grant thee thy Demetrius.
Keep word, Lysander; we must starve our sight
From lovers' food till morrow deep midnight.
Lysander
I will, my Hermia.   [*Exit* Hermia
                    Helena, adieu!
225 As you on him, Demetrius dote on you.
                              [*Exit* Lysander
Helena
How happy some o'er other some can be!
Through Athens I am thought as fair as she.
But what of that? Demetrius thinks not so;
He will not know what all but he do know.
230 And as he errs, doting on Hermia's eyes,
So I, admiring of his qualities.
Things base and vile, holding no quantity,
Love can transpose to form and dignity.
Love looks not with the eyes, but with the mind,
235 And therefore is wing'd Cupid painted blind.
Nor hath love's mind of any judgement taste;
Wings, and no eyes, figure unheedy haste;
And therefore is love said to be a child
Because in choice he is so oft beguil'd.
240 As waggish boys in game themselves forswear,
So the boy Love is perjur'd everywhere;

242 *ere*: until.
  eyne: eyes.

248 *intelligence*: piece of information.
249 *a dear expense*: The phrase has
  several meanings: (i) it will cost
  Demetrius some effort to give thanks
  to Helena, but (ii) thanks from
  Demetrius will be precious to Helena,
  even though (iii) she has paid a high
  price for them (in betraying her
  friends).

For, ere Demetrius looked on Hermia's eyne,
He hail'd down oaths that he was only mine,
And when this hail some heat from Hermia felt,
245 So he dissolv'd, and showers of oaths did melt.
I will go tell him of fair Hermia's flight:
Then to the wood will he, tomorrow night,
Pursue her; and for this intelligence,
If I have thanks it is a dear expense;
250 But herein mean I to enrich my pain,
To have his sight thither, and back again.   [*Exit*

Act 1 Scene 2
The first rehearsal of the tradesmen's play:
Quince must be diplomatic in handling
Nick Bottom, who wants to act all the parts
himself.

  0s.d. *Quince the Carpenter*: The names
    of these characters indicate their
    different trades—see 'Leading
    Characters in the Play', p.vii.

2–3 *You . . . scrip*: It was customary in
    Elizabethan plays for comic characters
    of low social status to speak in prose.
2 *generally*: Bottom tries to sound
    important—but he mistakes the
    meanings of words; here he should be
    saying 'severally' (= separately).
3 *scrip*: list.
5 *interlude*: play.

Scene 2

Athens, Peter Quince*'s house: enter* Quince *the
Carpenter, and* Snug *the Joiner, and* Bottom *the
Weaver, and* Flute *the Bellows-mender, and* Snout
the Tinker, and Starveling *the Tailor*

Quince
Is all our company here?
Bottom
You were best to call them generally, man by man,
according to the scrip.
Quince
Here is the scroll of every man's name which is thought
5 fit through all Athens to play in our interlude before the
duke and the duchess on his wedding day at night.

7 *treats on*: is about.

8–9 *grow to a point*: reach a conclusion.

10–11 *The most . . . Thisbe*:
Shakespeare parodies the elaborate
titles of some earlier Elizabethan
drama.

13–14 *by the scroll*: according to the list.

14 *spread yourselves*: sit down.
21 *look . . . eyes*: be prepared to shed
tears.
22 *condole*: lament.
in some measure: to a certain extent.
To the rest: now go on with the
business.
23 *my chief . . . tyrant*: I would prefer to
play a tyrant; I am best suited to the
part of a tyrant.
Ercles: Hercules, the superman of
Greek mythology.
24 *a part . . . split*: a part that demands
violent action and language.
25–32 *The . . . Fates*: These lines
burlesque the style of earlier verse
drama.
29 *Phibbus' car*: the chariot of the sun-
god, Phoebus Apollo.
32 *Fates*: the three sisters who (in
classical mythology) determined the
course of every man's life.
34 *vein*: style.
condoling: pathetic.
35 *bellows*: an instrument used to blow
air into organ pipes or (domestically)
on to coals to make the fire blaze.

Bottom

First, good Peter Quince, say what the play treats on;
then read the names of the actors; and so grow to a
point.

Quince

10   Marry, our play is 'The most lamentable comedy and
most cruel death of Pyramus and Thisbe'.

Bottom

A very good piece of work, I assure you, and a merry.
Now, good Peter Quince, call forth your actors by the
scroll. Masters, spread yourselves.

Quince

15   Answer as I call you. Nick Bottom, the weaver?

Bottom

Ready. Name what part I am for, and proceed.

Quince

You, Nick Bottom, are set down for Pyramus.

Bottom

What is Pyramus? A lover or a tyrant?

Quince

A lover that kills himself, most gallant, for love.

Bottom

20   That will ask some tears in the true performing of it. If I
do it, let the audience look to their eyes: I will move
storms, I will condole, in some measure. To the rest—
yet my chief humour is for a tyrant. I could play Ercles
rarely, or a part to tear a cat in, to make all split:

25   The raging rocks
         And shivering shocks
         Shall break the locks
             Of prison gates,
         And Phibbus' car
30   Shall shine from far,
         And make and mar
             The foolish Fates.

This was lofty. Now name the rest of the players.—This
is Ercles' vein, a tyrant's vein; a lover is more condoling.

Quince

35   Francis Flute, the bellows-mender?

Flute

Here, Peter Quince.

Quince

Flute, you must take Thisbe on you.

Flute

What is Thisbe? A wandering knight?

Quince

It is the lady that Pyramus must love.

Flute

40 Nay, faith, let not me play a woman: I have a beard coming.

Quince

That's all one: you shall play it in a mask, and you may speak as small as you will.

Bottom

And I may hide my face, let me play Thisbe too. I'll

45 speak in a monstrous little voice: 'Thisne, Thisne!'— 'Ah, Pyramus, my lover dear; thy Thisbe dear, and lady dear.'

Quince

No, no; you must play Pyramus; and Flute, you Thisbe.

Bottom

Well, proceed.

Quince

50 Robin Starveling, the tailor?

Starveling

Here, Peter Quince.

Quince

Robin Starveling, you must play Thisbe's mother. Tom Snout, the tinker?

Snout

Here, Peter Quince.

Quince

55 You, Pyramus' father; myself, Thisbe's father; Snug, the joiner, you the lion's part; and I hope here is a play fitted.

Snug

Have you the lion's part written? Pray you, if it be, give it me; for I am slow of study.

Quince

60 You may do it extempore; for it is nothing but roaring.

40 *faith*: by my faith.

42 *That's all one*: that doesn't matter.
mask: Fashionable ladies often wore masks to protect their complexions when they went out of doors.
43 *small*: shrill (like a woman's voice).
44 *And*: if.
45–7 *Thisne . . . dear*: Bottom tries to vary his voice, speaking as both Pyramus and Thisbe.

55 *Pyramus . . . father*: Neither of these characters appears in the final performance.
57 *fitted*: cast.

59 *slow of study*: a slow learner.

60 *extempore*: without a script, spontaneously.

61 *that*: so that.

64 *And*: if.
   fright: frighten.
65 *that*: so that.

69 *no more discretion*: Bottom wants to
   say 'no other choice'—but his words
   mean 'no more sense'.
70–1 *roar you*: roar for you.
71 *sucking dove*: Bottom confuses two
   models of gentleness—the sucking
   lamb and the *sitting* dove.
71–2 *and 'twere*: as though it were.
72 *nightingale*: a small bird that sings
   very sweetly in the evening.
74 *sweet-faced*: handsome.
   proper: masculine.
76 *must needs*: must certainly.

80 *discharge*: perform.

81 *in-grain*: deeply dyed.

82 *French-crown-colour*: light gold, the
   colour of a French coin.

84 *Some . . . at all*: some French men
   have bald heads; Quince is making a
   popular joke about the hair loss
   caused by syphilis (which the
   Elizabethans called 'the French
   disease').
86 *I am to*: I must.
87 *con*: learn.
88 *without*: outside.
90 *dogged*: followed.
   devices: plans.

Bottom

Let me play the lion too. I will roar that I will do any
man's heart good to hear me. I will roar that I will make
the duke say 'Let him roar again, let him roar again!'

Quince

And you should do it too terribly, you would fright the
65 duchess and the ladies that they would shriek; and that
were enough to hang us all.

All

That would hang us, every mother's son.

Bottom

I grant you, friends, if you should fright the ladies out of
their wits they would have no more discretion but to
70 hang us; but I will aggravate my voice so that I will roar
you as gently as any sucking dove. I will roar you and
'twere any nightingale.

Quince

You can play no part but Pyramus; for Pyramus is a
sweet-faced man, a proper man as one shall see in a
75 summer's day, a most lovely, gentlemanlike man:
therefore you must needs play Pyramus.

Bottom

Well, I will undertake it. What beard were I best to play
it in?

Quince

Why, what you will.

Bottom

80 I will discharge it in either your straw-colour beard,
your orange-tawny beard, your purple-in-grain beard,
or your French-crown-colour beard, your perfect
yellow.

Quince

Some of your French crowns have no hair at all, and
85 then you will play bare-faced. But, masters, here are
your parts, and I am to entreat you, request you, and
desire you to con them by tomorrow night, and meet
me in the palace wood, a mile without the town, by
moonlight; there will we rehearse, for if we meet in the
90 city we shall be dogged with company, and our devices

91 *bill*: list.
    properties: stage equipment.

94 *obscenely*: Bottom perhaps means
    'unseen', or 'seemly' (= properly).
    pains: care.
    be perfect: know your parts perfectly.
95 *adieu*: farewell (Bottom has learned a
    French word).
97 *hold . . . strings*: The meaning of this
    phrase is unknown, but Bottom
    appears to be saying that the actors
    must keep their promises ('hold'), or
    else be disgraced.

known. In the meantime I will draw a bill of properties, such as our play wants. I pray you, fail me not.

Bottom

We will meet, and there we may rehearse most obscenely and courageously. Take pains, be perfect:
95 adieu!

Quince

At the duke's oak we meet.

Bottom

Enough; hold, or cut bowstrings. [*Exeunt*

ACT 2

Act 2 Scene 1

Oberon and Titania have quarrelled, and Oberon, planning his revenge, sends Puck to get the magic flower—which can also be used to help Helena.

Os.d. *at one door*: from one side of the stage.
2 *dale*: valley.
3 *Thorough*: an old form of 'through' (retained here for the sake of the rhythm).
briar: thorn.
4 *pale*: piece of land enclosed by fencing.
7 *moon's sphere*: the orbit of the moon.
9 *dew*: sprinkle with dew.
her orbs: circles of rich grass, thought to be formed by the dancing of fairies.
10 *The cowslips tall*: Cowslips are wild flowers (with red spots in yellow, bell-shaped heads) about 15cm high—which is 'tall' from a fairy's point of view; 'tall' also meant 'brave', 'handsome'.
pensioners: The Gentlemen of the Royal Bodyguard in Queen Elizabeth's court (who wore red and gold uniforms) were known as 'pensioners'.
12 *favours*: gifts.
13 *savours*: scents, fragrance.
16 *lob of spirits*: peasant fairy; see 'Leading Characters in the Play', p.vii.
17 *anon*: very soon.

SCENE 1

A wood near Athens: enter a Fairy *at one door, and* Puck *at another*

Puck
How now, spirit; whither wander you?
    Fairy
Over hill, over dale,
    Thorough bush, thorough briar,
Over park, over pale,
    Thorough flood, thorough fire;   5
I do wander everywhere
Swifter than the moon's sphere;
And I serve the Fairy Queen,
To dew her orbs upon the green.
The cowslips tall her pensioners be;   10
In their gold coats spots you see—
Those be rubies, fairy favours,
In those freckles live their savours.
    I must go seek some dewdrops here,
    And hang a pearl in every cowslip's ear.   15
Farewell, thou lob of spirits; I'll be gone.
Our queen and all her elves come here anon.

Puck
The king doth keep his revels here tonight.
Take heed the queen come not within his sight,
20 For Oberon is passing fell and wrath,
Because that she as her attendant hath
A lovely boy stol'n from an Indian king;
She never had so sweet a changeling,
And jealous Oberon would have the child
25 Knight of his train, to trace the forests wild.
But she perforce withholds the loved boy,
Crowns him with flowers, and makes him all her joy.
And now they never meet in grove or green,
By fountain clear or spangl'd starlight sheen,
30 But they do square, that all their elves for fear
Creep into acorn cups and hide them there.
Fairy
Either I mistake your shape and making quite,
Or else you are that shrewd and knavish sprite
Called Robin Goodfellow. Are not you he
35 That frights the maidens of the villagery,
Skim milk, and sometimes labour in the quern,
And bootless make the breathless housewife churn,
And sometime make the drink to bear no barm,
Mislead night-wanderers, laughing at their harm?
40 Those that 'Hobgoblin' call you, and 'Sweet Puck',
You do their work, and they shall have good luck.
Are not you he?

19 *heed*: care.
20 *passing*: extremely.
   fell: fierce.
23 *changeling*: child (usually ugly or stupid) left by the fairies in exchange for a beautiful human baby.
24 *jealous*: envious.
25 *Knight of his train*: to be a knight in his service.
   trace: roam through.
26 *perforce*: forcibly.
   loved: lovèd.
29 *sheen*: shining.
30 *square*: quarrel.
   that: so that.
31 *acorn cups*: The cup-shaped holder of the acorn is less than 2cm in diameter.
32 *making*: appearance.
   quite: completely.
34 *Robin Goodfellow*: See 'Leading Characters in the Play', p.viii.
34–6 *Are . . . milk*: In these lines Puck is both 'he' and 'you'.
35 *villagery*: village people.
36 *Skim milk*: take the cream from the milk.
   quern: churn (in which milk is violently stirred to make butter).
37 *bootless*: without result.
38 *barm*: froth.
39 *Mislead*: Puck demonstrates this skill in *Act 3*, Scenes 1 and 2.

Puck

Thou speakest aright;

I am that merry wanderer of the night.

I jest to Oberon, and make him smile

45 When I a fat and bean-fed horse beguile,

Neighing in likeness of a filly foal;

And sometime lurk I in a gossip's bowl

In very likeness of a roasted crab,

And when she drinks, against her lips I bob,

50 And on her wither'd dewlap pour the ale.

The wisest aunt, telling the saddest tale,

Sometime for threefoot stool mistaketh me;

Then slip I from her bum, down topples she,

And 'Tailor' cries, and falls into a cough;

55 And then the whole choir hold their hips and loffe,

And waxen in their mirth, and neeze, and swear

A merrier hour was never wasted there.

But room, fairy: here comes Oberon.

Fairy

And here my mistress. Would that he were gone!

Enter Oberon, the King of Fairies, at one door, with his train; and Titania, the Queen, at another with hers

Oberon

60 Ill met by moonlight, proud Titania!

Titania

What, jealous Oberon? Fairies, skip hence.

I have forsworn his bed and company.

Oberon

Tarry, rash wanton! Am not I thy lord?

Titania

Then I must be thy lady. But I know

65 When thou hast stol'n away from Fairyland,

And in the shape of Corin sat all day

Playing on pipes of corn, and versing love

To amorous Phillida. Why art thou here

Come from the farthest step of India?—

70 But that, forsooth, the bouncing Amazon,

Your buskin'd mistress and your warrior love,

---

44 *jest to Oberon*: am Oberon's jester.

46 *filly*: female.

47 *gossip*: old woman.

48 *very*: true.
   crab: crab apple (used as a spice in warmed ale).

50 *dewlap*: the folds of skin hanging round an old person's throat.

51 *aunt*: old woman.

52 *threefoot*: three-legged.

54 *Tailor*: cheat.
   falls into a cough: starts coughing.

55 *choir*: company.
   loffe: laugh; Puck imitates the language of peasants.

56 *waxen*: increase.
   neeze: sneeze.

57 *wasted*: spent.

58 *room*: make room.

59 *Would*: I wish.

60 *Ill met*: an unlucky meeting; rhyming couplets give way to blank verse when Oberon meets Titania.

61 *jealous*: envious.

62 *forsworn*: refused.

63 *Tarry*: wait.
   rash wanton: headstrong, wilful creature.
   lord: husband (and therefore entitled to respect from his wife).

64 *lady*: wife (and therefore entitled to expect faithfulness from her husband).

66 *in . . . Phillida*: behaved like one of those shepherds in pastoral poetry singing to his lady-love; Oberon, being a spirit, would need to assume human form in order to have any conversation with a mortal.

67 *pipes of corn*: corn-stalks used as musical pipes.

69 *step*: hill (perhaps the Himalayas).

70 *But that, forsooth*: only, indeed, because.
   the bouncing Amazon: i.e. Hippolyta; see 'Leading Characters in the Play', p.vii.

71 *buskin'd*: wearing high boots.

73 *give their bed*: bless their union with.
75 *Glance at*: make rude remarks about.
78–80 *From . . . Antiopa*: Little is known about three of these women except that Theseus deserted all of them! Ariadne helped him to find his way through the labyrinth on his expedition to kill the Minotaur.
78 *ravished*: ravishèd.
81 *forgeries*: falsehoods.
82 *middle summer's spring*: beginning of midsummer period.
83 *dale*: valley.
   mead: meadow.
84 *paved fountain*: pavèd; fountain with small pebbles at the bottom.
   rushy brook: small stream with tall rushes growing at the sides.
85 *beached*: beachèd.
   margent: margin, edge.
86 *ringlets*: dances round the fairy rings (see line 9note).
   whistling wind: the wind whistled as music for their dancing.
87 *brawls*: quarrels.
   sport: entertainment.
88 *in vain*: uselessly.
90 *Contagious*: carrying diseases.
91 *pelting*: paltry.
92 *overborne their continents*: flooded over their banks.
93 *The ox . . . vain*: the ploughing has been useless.
94 *lost his sweat*: wasted his effort.
   green: unripe; ripe corn has hanging tendrils, like a man's beard.
95 *ere*: before.

To Theseus must be wedded; and you come
To give their bed joy and prosperity.
    Oberon
How canst thou thus, for shame, Titania,
75 Glance at my credit with Hippolyta,
Knowing I know thy love to Theseus?
Didst not thou lead him through the glimmering night
From Perigenia, whom he ravished,
And make him with fair Aegles break his faith,
80 With Ariadne, and Antiopa?
    Titania
These are the forgeries of jealousy:
And never since the middle summer's spring
Met we on hill, in dale, forest, or mead,
By paved fountain or by rushy brook,
85 Or in the beached margent of the sea
To dance our ringlets to the whistling wind,
But with thy brawls thou hast disturb'd our sport.
Therefore the winds, piping to us in vain,
As in revenge have suck'd up from the sea
90 Contagious fogs; which, falling in the land,
Hath every pelting river made so proud
That they have overborne their continents.
The ox hath therefore stretch'd his yoke in vain,
The ploughman lost his sweat, and the green corn
95 Hath rotted ere his youth attain'd a beard.

96 *drowned*: drownèd.
97 *fatted*: grown fat.
   murrion flock: sheep and cattle.
98 *nine-men's-morris*: A game played
   with nine pins or stones on specially
   marked ground.
99 *quaint*: intricate; the maze was a
   popular feature of Elizabethan
   gardens.
   wanton green: overgrown grass.
101 *want*: are deprived of.
   cheer: festivities.
103 *governess of floods*: The moon is
   partly responsible for the tides.
104 *washes*: It was thought that the moon
   shed moisture on the earth.
105 *rheumatic . . . abound*: there are a lot
   of colds and sniffles about; ('rheum' =
   a watery discharge from eyes and
   nose).
106 *thorough*: through.
   distemperature: disturbance in the
   temperature of the weather.
107 *hoary-headed frosts*: frosts covering
   everything with white.
109 *Hiems*: winter (personified as an old
   man).
110 *odorous*: scented.
   chaplet: wreath worn on the head.
111 *as in mockery*: as though making fun
   of the old man.
112 *childing*: fruitful (bearing children).
113 *wonted liveries*: usual uniforms.
   mazed: mazèd; bewildered.
114 *By . . . which*: cannot distinguish the
   seasons by their produce.
115 *progeny*: offspring.
116 *debate*: arguing.
117 *original*: origin.
118 *Do . . . it*: you make it better.
   it lies in you: it is in your power.
119 *cross*: disobey.
120 *but*: only.
121 *henchman*: page.
   Set . . . rest: be assured.
122 *of*: from.
123 *a votress . . . order*: a nun vowed to
   serve me.
124 *spiced*: spicèd; fragrant.
126 *Neptune*: god of the sea.
127 *Marking*: observing.
   embarked . . . flood: embarkèd;
   merchant ships on the tide bringing
   them to shore.

The fold stands empty in the drowned field,
And crows are fatted with the murrion flock;
The nine-men's-morris is filled up with mud,
And the quaint mazes in the wanton green
100 For lack of tread are undistinguishable.
The human mortals want their winter cheer;
No night is now with hymn or carol bless'd.
Therefore the moon, the governess of floods,
Pale in her anger, washes all the air,
105 That rheumatic diseases do abound;
And thorough this distemperature we see
The seasons alter; hoary-headed frosts
Fall in the fresh lap of the crimson rose,
And on old Hiems' thin and icy crown
110 An odorous chaplet of sweet summer buds
Is, as in mockery, set. The spring, the summer,
The childing autumn, angry winter change
Their wonted liveries, and the mazed world
By their increase now knows not which is which.
115 And this same progeny of evils comes
From our debate, from our dissension.
We are their parents and original.

Oberon
Do you amend it, then: it lies in you.
Why should Titania cross her Oberon?
120 I do but beg a little changeling boy
To be my henchman.

Titania
                        Set your heart at rest.
The fairy land buys not the child of me.
His mother was a votress of my order,
And in the spiced Indian air by night
125 Full often hath she gossip'd by my side,
And sat with me on Neptune's yellow sands
Marking th'embarked traders on the flood,
When we have laugh'd to see the sails conceive
And grow big-bellied with the wanton wind;
130 Which she, with pretty and with swimming gait
Following (her womb then rich with my young
    squire),
Would imitate, and sail upon the land

'We shall chide downright if I longer stay.' (*2*, 1, 145) Stella Gonet as Titania and Alex Jennings as Oberon, Royal Shakespeare Company, 1995.

128 *conceive*: swell (as though pregnant).
129 *wanton*: playful, amorous.
130 *swimming*: gliding.
    gait: movement.
131 *Following*: copying.
    rich: pregnant.
    squire: gentleman (especially one who
    attends a lady).
135 *of that boy*: giving birth to the boy.
138 *intend you stay*: do you intend to stay?
139 *Perchance*: perhaps.
140 *round*: circular dance—compare
    'ringlets' (line 86).

146 *not from*: not go from.
147 *injury*: insult.

149 *Since once*: the time when.
    promontory: piece of land jutting out
    into the sea.
151 *dulcet*: sweet-sounding.
    breath: song.
152 *rude*: rough (badly behaved).
    civil: calm (well behaved).
153 *spheres*: orbits.

155 *very*: same.
158 *vestal*: virgin; the Roman Vestal
    Virgins vowed eternal virginity, in
    service to Vesta, goddess of the home.
    throned: thronèd.
159 *loveshaft*: arrow of love.
160 *As it*: as though it.
161 *might*: was able to.
    fiery: i.e. because it produced the
    fires of love.
162 *chaste*: Diana, goddess of the moon,
    was also goddess of chastity and
    protector of virginity.
163 *imperial votress*: royal lady who has
    taken vows.
    passed: passèd.

To fetch me trifles, and return again
As from a voyage, rich with merchandise.
135 But she, being mortal, of that boy did die,
And for her sake do I rear up her boy;
And for her sake I will not part with him.
        Oberon
How long within this wood intend you stay?
        Titania
Perchance till after Theseus' wedding day.
140 If you will patiently dance in our round,
And see our moonlight revels, go with us:
If not, shun me, and I will spare your haunts.
        Oberon
Give me that boy, and I will go with thee.
        Titania
Not for thy fairy kingdom! Fairies, away.
145 We shall chide downright if I longer stay.
                    [*Exeunt* Titania *and her train*
        Oberon
Well, go thy way. Thou shalt not from this grove
Till I torment thee for this injury.
My gentle Puck, come hither. Thou rememberest
Since once I sat upon a promontory,
150 And heard a mermaid on a dolphin's back
Uttering such dulcet and harmonious breath
That the rude sea grew civil at her song,
And certain stars shot madly from their spheres
To hear the sea-maid's music?
        Puck
                        I remember.
        Oberon
155 That very time I saw (but thou couldst not)
Flying between the cold moon and the earth
Cupid all arm'd: a certain aim he took
At a fair vestal throned by the west,
And loos'd his loveshaft smartly from his bow
160 As it should pierce a hundred thousand hearts;
But I might see young Cupid's fiery shaft
Quench'd in the chaste beams of the watery moon;
And the imperial votress passed on
In maiden meditation, fancy-free.

165 *mark'd*: observed.
  bolt: arrow.

168 *love-in-idleness*: The flower is the pansy—but the myth is Shakespeare's own creation.

171 *or . . . or*: either . . . or.

174 *Ere*: before.
  leviathan: whale.
  league: measurement of distance (about three miles).
175 *put a girdle*: encircle.

181 *busy*: mischievous.

186 *I am invisible*: Oberon probably throws a black cloak around himself.
187 *conference*: conversation.

165 Yet mark'd I where the bolt of Cupid fell:
It fell upon a little western flower,
Before, milk-white; now purple with love's wound:
And maidens call it 'love-in-idleness'.
Fetch me that flower, the herb I show'd thee once;
170 The juice of it on sleeping eyelids laid
Will make or man or woman madly dote
Upon the next live creature that it sees.
Fetch me this herb, and be thou here again
Ere the leviathan can swim a league.
    Puck
175 I'll put a girdle round about the earth
In forty minutes! [*Exit*
    Oberon
                Having once this juice
I'll watch Titania when she is asleep,
And drop the liquor of it in her eyes:
The next thing then she, waking, looks upon—
180 Be it on lion, bear, or wolf, or bull,
On meddling monkey, or on busy ape—
She shall pursue it with the soul of love.
And ere I take this charm from off her sight
(As I can take it with another herb)
185 I'll make her render up her page to me.
But who comes here? I am invisible,
And I will overhear their conference.

Enter Demetrius, Helena *following him*

Demetrius

I love thee not, therefore pursue me not.
Where is Lysander, and fair Hermia?
190 The one I'll slay, the other slayeth me.
Thou told'st me they were stol'n unto this wood,
And here am I, and wood within this wood
Because I cannot meet my Hermia.
Hence, get thee gone, and follow me no more.

Helena

195 You draw me, you hard-hearted adamant!
But yet you draw not iron, for my heart
Is true as steel. Leave you your power to draw,
And I shall have no power to follow you.

Demetrius

Do I entice you? Do I speak you fair?
200 Or rather do I not in plainest truth
Tell you I do not, nor I cannot love you?

Helena

And even for that do I love you the more.
I am your spaniel; and, Demetrius,
The more you beat me I will fawn on you.
205 Use me but as your spaniel: spurn me, strike me,
Neglect me, lose me; only give me leave,
Unworthy as I am, to follow you.
What worser place can I beg in your love
(And yet a place of high respect with me)
210 Than to be used as you use your dog?

Demetrius

Tempt not too much the hatred of my spirit;
For I am sick when I do look on thee.

Helena

And I am sick when I look not on you.

Demetrius

You do impeach your modesty too much,
215 To leave the city and commit yourself
Into the hands of one that loves you not;
To trust the opportunity of night,

190 *slayeth me*: i.e. because she refuses to love him.
191 *stol'n*: escaped.
192 *and wood*: and mad.

195 *draw*: attract.
    adamant: magnet.

197 *Leave you*: if you will give up.

199 *speak you fair*: say kind words to you.
203 *spaniel*: This breed of dog has a reputation for faithfulness, even when treated badly.

204 *fawn*: cringe, beg for favour.
205 *spurn*: kick.
210 *used*: usèd.

214 *impeach your modesty*: cause your modesty to be suspected.

217–19 *To trust . . . virginity*: to trust that your precious virginity will be safe when the night gives opportunity and the lonely place offers temptation.

And the ill counsel of a desert place,
With the rich worth of your virginity.
Helena
220 Your virtue is my privilege: for that
It is not night when I do see your face,
Therefore I think I am not in the night;
Nor doth this wood lack worlds of company,
For you, in my respect, are all the world.
225 Then how can it be said I am alone
When all the world is here to look on me?
Demetrius
I'll run from thee and hide me in the brakes,
And leave thee to the mercy of wild beasts.
Helena
The wildest hath not such a heart as you.
230 Run when you will: the story shall be chang'd;
Apollo flies, and Daphne holds the chase,
The dove pursues the griffin, the mild hind
Makes speed to catch the tiger—bootless speed,
When cowardice pursues, and valour flies!
Demetrius
235 I will not stay thy questions. Let me go;
Or if thou follow me, do not believe
But I shall do thee mischief in the wood.
Helena
Ay, in the temple, in the town, the field,
You do me mischief. Fie, Demetrius,
240 Your wrongs do set a scandal on my sex!
We cannot fight for love, as men may do;
We should be woo'd, and were not made to woo.
[*Exit* Demetrius
I'll follow thee, and make a heaven of hell,
To die upon the hand I love so well.   [*Exit*
Oberon
245 Fare thee well, nymph. Ere he do leave this grove
Thou shalt fly him, and he shall seek thy love.

220 *virtue*: particular nature.
privilege: protection.
for that: because.

224 *respect*: opinion.

227 *brakes*: bushes.

231 *Apollo . . . chase*: Apollo chased after Daphne, but she prayed to Diana for protection—and was changed into a laurel tree; the story is told in Ovid's *Metamorphoses*.
232 *griffin*: a fabulous monster, with head and wings of an eagle and the body of a man.
hind: female deer.
233 *bootless*: useless.
235 *stay your questions*: wait to hear your arguments.
237 *But*: but that.
do thee mischief: harm you.

240 *wrongs*: ill-treatment.
set . . . sex: make me act in a way that is improper for a woman.

245 *nymph*: girl.
246 *fly him*: run away from him.

249 *wild thyme*: a low-growing scented
     herb with tiny purple flowers.
     blows: blossoms.
250 *oxlips*: flowers slightly bigger than
     cowslips.
251 *woodbine*: honeysuckle, a climbing
     plant that makes a shelter (canopy)
     over the bank.
252 *musk-roses*: these also climb, and are
     heavily scented.
     eglantine: another kind of wild rose.
253 *sometime*: at some time or other.
254 *Lull'd*: sent to sleep.
255 *throws*: sheds (when it is out-grown).
     enamell'd: coloured (and smooth).
256 *Weed wide enough*: a garment that is
     wide enough.

267 *cock crow*: The crowing of the cock is
     usually the signal for supernatural
     beings to leave the world of mortals—
     though Oberon will say, later in the
     play (*3, 2, 388*), that he and the other
     fairies are not confined to the hours of
     darkness.

Act 2 Scene 2
Titania sleeps, and Oberon anoints her eyes
with the juice of his flower. Puck, mistaking
him for Demetrius, sprinkles juice on
Lysander's eyes—who wakes up and finds
himself in love with Helena.

1 *roundel*: dance in a circle.
2 *third . . . minute*: This is the speed of
   fairy life!
3 *cankers*: small worms.
4 *war*: fight.
   reremice: bats.

Enter Puck

Hast thou the flower there? Welcome, wanderer.
  Puck
Ay, there it is.
    Oberon
              I pray thee give it me.
I know a bank where the wild thyme blows,
250 Where oxlips and the nodding violet grows,
Quite overcanopied with luscious woodbine,
With sweet musk-roses, and with eglantine:
There sleeps Titania sometime of the night,
Lull'd in these flowers with dances and delight;
255 And there the snake throws her enamell'd skin,
Weed wide enough to wrap a fairy in;
And with the juice of this I'll streak her eyes,
And make her full of hateful fantasies.
Take thou some of it, and seek through this grove:
260 A sweet Athenian lady is in love
With a disdainful youth; anoint his eyes,
But do it when the next thing he espies
May be the lady. Thou shalt know the man
By the Athenian garments he hath on.
265 Effect it with some care, that he may prove
More fond on her than she upon her love.
And look thou meet me ere the first cock crow.
  Puck
Fear not, my lord; your servant shall do so.   [*Exeunt*

SCENE 2

Another part of the wood: enter Titania, *Queen of
Fairies, with her train*

Titania
Come, now a roundel and a fairy song,
Then for the third part of a minute, hence—
Some to kill cankers in the musk-rose buds,
Some war with reremice for their leathern wings
5 To make my small elves coats, and some keep back

The clamorous owl that nightly hoots and wonders
At our quaint spirits. Sing me now asleep;
Then to your offices, and let me rest.

Fairies *sing*

First Fairy
You spotted snakes with double tongue,
10   Thorny hedgehogs, be not seen.
Newts and blindworms, do no wrong,
    Come not near our Fairy Queen.
Chorus
    Philomel with melody
    Sing in our sweet lullaby,
15   Lulla, lulla, lullaby; lulla, lulla, lullaby.
        Never harm
        Nor spell nor charm
        Come our lovely lady nigh.
        So good night, with lullaby.
First Fairy
20   Weaving spiders, come not here;
        Hence, you longlegg'd spinners, hence!
Beetles black approach not near;
        Worm nor snail, do no offence.
Chorus
        Philomel with melody
25   Sing in our sweet lullaby,
Lulla, lulla, lullaby; lulla, lulla, lullaby.
        Never harm
        Nor spell nor charm
        Come our lovely lady nigh.
30   So good night, with lullaby.

Titania *sleeps*

Second Fairy
Hence, away! Now all is well;
One aloof stand sentinel!   [*Exeunt* Fairies

---

7 *quaint*: dainty.

8 *to your offices*: go and do your duties.

9 *double*: forked.

11 *Newts and blindworms*: The Elizabethans (wrongly) believed these to be poisonous.

13 *Philomel*: The nymph Philomela was transformed into a nightingale after being raped by Tereus (another story told in Ovid's *Metamorphoses*).

18 *nigh*: near to.

20 *spiders*: The Elizabethans believed that these were all poisonous.

30s.d. *Titania sleeps*: Titania does not wake until *3, 1, 113*—perhaps remaining in view of the audience, or concealed by a curtain which is closed by the fairies, opened and then closed again by Oberon when he departs at line 40.

32 *stand sentinel*: keep guard.

Enter Oberon; *he squeezes the juice on* Titania's *eyes*

Oberon
What thou seest when thou dost wake,
Do it for thy true love take;
35 Love and languish for his sake.
Be it ounce or cat or bear,
Pard, or boar with bristled hair
In thy eye that shall appear
When thou wak'st, it is thy dear.
40 Wake when some vile thing is near!

[*Exit*

Enter Lysander *and* Hermia

Lysander
Fair love, you faint with wandering in the wood,
    And, to speak truth, I have forgot our way.
We'll rest us, Hermia, if you think it good,
    And tarry for the comfort of the day.
Hermia
45 Be it so, Lysander; find you out a bed,
For I upon this bank will rest my head.
Lysander
One turf shall serve as pillow for us both;
One heart, one bed, two bosoms, and one troth.
Hermia
Nay, good Lysander, for my sake, my dear,
50 Lie further off yet; do not lie so near.
Lysander
O take the sense, sweet, of my innocence!
Love takes the meaning in love's conference;
I mean that my heart unto yours is knit,
So that but one heart we can make of it:
55 Two bosoms interchained with an oath,
So then two bosoms and a single troth.
Then by your side no bed-room me deny,
For lying so, Hermia, I do not lie.
Hermia
Lysander riddles very prettily.

36 *ounce*: lynx.
37 *Pard*: leopard.

44 *tarry*: wait.

48 *troth*: truth.

50 *further off yet*: still further away from.

51 *take . . . innocence*: understand my innocent meaning.
52 *Love . . . conference*: love gives a generous interpretation to what is being said in the conversation of lovers.
53 *knit*: inextricably joined together.
54 *but one*: only one.
55 *interchained*: interchainèd; linked.
56 *troth*: bond of love.
58 *lying . . . lie*: sleeping next to you like this I would not be deceiving you; Lysander puns on the different senses of 'lie'.
59 *riddles*: plays with words.
    prettily: cleverly.

60 *much beshrew*: I really curse (Hermia is only half-serious).
61 *lied*: told a lie.
62 *for*: for the sake of.

66 *So far be distant*: keep just so far away.

74 *approve*: test.
75 *force . . . love*: power to awaken love.

77 *Weeds*: garments.
78 *he my master said*: the man that my master said.
79 *Despised*: despisèd.

82 *durst*: dares.
83 *lack-love*: man who does not love her. *kill-courtesy*: one whose rudeness destroys courtesy.
84 *Churl*: brute.

86-7 *let . . . eyelid*: may love prevent sleep from settling on his eyes.

60 Now much beshrew my manners and my pride
If Hermia meant to say Lysander lied.
But, gentle friend, for love and courtesy
Lie further off, in human modesty;
Such separation as may well be said
65 Becomes a virtuous bachelor and a maid,
So far be distant, and good night, sweet friend;
Thy love ne'er alter till thy sweet life end!
    Lysander
Amen, amen, to that fair prayer say I,
And then end life when I end loyalty!
70 Here is my bed; sleep give thee all his rest.
    Hermia
With half that wish the wisher's eyes be press'd.

They sleep

Enter Puck

Puck
Through the forest have I gone,
But Athenian found I none
On whose eyes I might approve
75 This flower's force in stirring love.
Night and silence—Who is here?
Weeds of Athens he doth wear:
This is he my master said
Despised the Athenian maid;
80 And here the maiden, sleeping sound
On the dank and dirty ground.
Pretty soul, she durst not lie
Near this lack-love, this kill-courtesy.
Churl, upon thy eyes I throw
85 All the power this charm doth owe.
[*He squeezes the juice on* Lysander's *eyes*]
When thou wak'st let love forbid
Sleep his seat on thy eyelid.
So, awake when I am gone;
For I must now to Oberon.   [*Exit*

Enter Demetrius *and* Helena, *running*

Helena

90 Stay, though thou kill me, sweet Demetrius!

Demetrius

91 *charge thee, hence*: command you to
go away.
haunt: pursue.
92 *darkling*: in the dark.

I charge thee, hence, and do not haunt me thus.

Helena

O wilt thou darkling leave me? Do not so!

Demetrius

Stay, on thy peril; I alone will go.   [*Exit*

Helena

94 *fond*: foolish.

O, I am out of breath in this fond chase!

95 *the . . . grace*: the less favour do I
receive.

95 The more my prayer, the lesser is my grace.
Happy is Hermia, wheresoe'er she lies,

97 *blessed*: blessèd.

For she hath blessed and attractive eyes.
How came her eyes so bright? Not with salt tears—
If so, my eyes are oftener wash'd than hers.

100 No, no, I am as ugly as a bear,
For beasts that meet me run away for fear.
Therefore no marvel though Demetrius

103 *as a monster*: as though I were a
monster.
104 *glass*: mirror.
105 *sphery eyne*: starlike eyes.

Do as a monster fly my presence thus.
What wicked and dissembling glass of mine

105 Made me compare with Hermia's sphery eyne?
But who is here?—Lysander, on the ground?
Dead, or asleep? I see no blood, no wound.
Lysander, if you live, good sir, awake!

Lysander

[*Waking*] And run through fire I will for thy sweet sake!

110 *Transparent*: glorious; Lysander
proceeds to play on the more usual
meaning (= able to be seen through).
art: magic.

110 Transparent Helena, nature shows art
That through thy bosom makes me see thy heart.
Where is Demetrius? O, how fit a word
Is that vile name to perish on my sword!

Helena

Do not say so, Lysander, say not so.

115 *what though*: what does it matter.

115 What though he love your Hermia? Lord, what though?
Yet Hermia still loves you; then be content.

Lysander

Content with Hermia? No; I do repent
The tedious minutes I with her have spent.
Not Hermia, but Helena I love.

121 *The will . . . sway'd*: a man's heart is
ruled by reason.

124 *till . . . reason*: was not mature in
judgement until now.
125 *touching . . . skill*: having reached the
height of discrimination.
126 *marshall*: director.
will: desire.
127 *o'erlook*: read over.
128 *love's richest book*: i.e. the eyes of a
woman; Shakespeare frequently plays
with this image.
129 *Wherefore*: why.
keen: cruel.

134 *insufficiency*: unattractiveness.

135 *Good troth*: indeed.
good sooth: really.

137 *perforce*: indeed.

138 *gentleness*: courtesy.

139 *of*: by.

143 *surfeit of*: over-indulgence in.

145–6 *the heresies . . . deceive*: false
beliefs, now renounced, are hated
most by those who once believed
them.
148 *of me*: by me.
149 *address*: apply.

156 *prey*: act of preying on something.

120 Who will not change a raven for a dove?
The will of man is by his reason sway'd,
And reason says you are the worthier maid.
Things growing are not ripe until their season;
So I, being young, till now ripe not to reason.
125 And touching now the point of human skill,
Reason becomes the marshal to my will.
And leads me to your eyes, where I o'erlook
Love's stories written in love's richest book.
    Helena
Wherefore was I to this keen mockery born?
130 When at your hands did I deserve this scorn?
Is't not enough, is't not enough, young man,
That I did never, no, nor never can
Deserve a sweet look from Demetrius' eye
But you must flout my insufficiency?
135 Good troth, you do me wrong, good sooth, you do,
In such disdainful manner me to woo!
But fare you well: perforce I must confess
I thought you lord of more true gentleness.
O, that a lady of one man refus'd
140 Should of another therefore be abus'd!   [*Exit*
    Lysander
She sees not Hermia. Hermia, sleep thou there,
And never mayst thou come Lysander near.
For, as a surfeit of the sweetest things
The deepest loathing to the stomach brings,
145 Or as the heresies that men do leave
Are hated most of those they did deceive,
So thou, my surfeit and my heresy,
Of all be hated, but the most of me!
And, all my powers, address your love and might
150 To honour Helen, and to be her knight.   [*Exit*
    Hermia
[*Waking*] Help me, Lysander, help me! Do thy best
To pluck this crawling serpent from my breast!
Ay me, for pity! What a dream was here!
Lysander, look how I do quake with fear—
155 Methought a serpent ate my heart away,
And you sat smiling at his cruel prey.

157 *remov'd*: gone away.

159 *and if*: if.
160 *of all loves*: for love's sake.
161 *nigh*: near.

Lysander! What, remov'd? Lysander, lord!
What, out of hearing? Gone? No sound, no word?
Alack, where are you? Speak and if you hear.
160 Speak, of all loves! I swoon almost with fear.
No? Then I well perceive you are not nigh.
Either death or you I'll find immediately.   [*Exit*

ACT 3

Act 3 Scene 1
The tradesmen discuss some staging problems, then begin to rehearse their play. Puck interrupts, puts a false head on Bottom, and leads him to Titania—who immediately falls in love.

2 *Pat, pat*: most punctually.

4 *brake*: bush; hawthorn is a thick shrub with small white flowers.
tiring-house: dressing-room.
4–5 *in action*: with gestures and movements.

10 *abide*: endure.

12 *By'r lakin*: by Our Lady.
parlous: terrible.

14 *Not a whit*: not at all.
14–15 *Write me a prologue*: just you write a prologue; 'me' here is only for emphasis.

21 *eight and six*: alternating lines of eight and six syllables; the usual ballad metre (compare Bottom's song, lines 109–17).

SCENE 1

The wood: enter the Clowns, Bottom, Quince, Snout, Starveling, Snug, *and* Flute. Titania *remains on stage, asleep*

Bottom
Are we all met?
Quince
Pat, pat; and here's a marvellous convenient place for our rehearsal. This green plot shall be our stage, this hawthorn brake our tiring-house, and we will do it in
5 action as we will do it before the duke.
Bottom
Peter Quince!
Quince
What sayest thou, bully Bottom?
Bottom
There are things in this comedy of Pyramus and Thisbe that will never please. First, Pyramus must draw a sword
10 to kill himself, which the ladies cannot abide. How answer you that?
Snout
By'r lakin, a parlous fear!
Starveling
I believe we must leave the killing out, when all is done.
Bottom
Not a whit; I have a device to make all well. Write me a
15 prologue, and let the prologue seem to say we will do no harm with our swords, and that Pyramus is not killed indeed; and for the more better assurance, tell them that I, Pyramus, am not Pyramus, but Bottom the weaver: this will put them out of fear.
Quince
20 Well, we will have such a prologue; and it shall be written in eight and six.

Bottom

No, make it two more: let it be written in eight and eight.

Snout

Will not the ladies be afeard of the lion?

Starveling

25 I fear it, I promise you.

Bottom

Masters, you ought to consider with yourself, to bring in (God shield us!) a lion among ladies is a most dreadful thing; for there is not a more fearful wildfowl than your lion living; and we ought to look to't.

Snout

30 Therefore another prologue must tell he is not a lion.

Bottom

Nay, you must name his name, and half his face must be seen through the lion's neck, and he himself must speak through, saying thus, or to the same defect: 'Ladies', or 'Fair ladies, I would wish you', or 'I would request you', 35 or 'I would entreat you, not to fear, not to tremble: my life for yours. If you think I come hither as a lion, it were pity of my life. No, I am no such thing; I am a man, as other men are'—and there indeed let him name his name, and tell them plainly he is Snug the joiner.

Quince

40 Well, it shall be so. But there is two hard things: that is, to bring the moonlight into a chamber; for, you know, Pyramus and Thisbe meet by moonlight.

Snug

Doth the moon shine that night we play our play?

Bottom

A calendar, a calendar! Look in the almanac—find out 45 moonshine, find out moonshine!

Quince

Yes, it doth shine that night.

Bottom

Why, then may you leave a casement of the great chamber window, where we play, open, and the moon may shine in at the casement.

33 *defect*: Bottom means 'effect'.

36–7 *it were . . . life*: my life would be in danger (he would have to ask for pity).

47 *casement*: window.

50 *a bush of thorns*: Ancient legends tell of a man who broke the religious laws by gathering sticks on the Jewish sabbath (or Christian Sunday), and was punished by being banished to the moon.
51 *disfigure*: Quince means 'figure' (= represent).

58 *loam*: mixture of clay, sand, and straw—used for making bricks.
rough-cast: mixture of lime and gravel (used in plastering outside walls).

61–2 *every mother's son*: every one of us.

65 *hempen homespuns*: coarse country folk (wearing homespun clothes made of hemp).
67 *toward*: in preparation.
auditor: member of the audience.

70 *odious*: hateful.
savours: perfumes.

Quince
50 Ay; or else one must come in with a bush of thorns and a lantern, and say he comes to disfigure, or to present the person of Moonshine. Then there is another thing: we must have a wall in the great chamber; for Pyramus and Thisbe, says the story, did talk through the chink of
55 a wall.
Snout
You can never bring in a wall. What say you, Bottom?
Bottom
Some man or other must present Wall; and let him have some plaster, or some loam, or some rough-cast about him to signify Wall; or let him hold his fingers thus, and
60 through that cranny shall Pyramus and Thisbe whisper.
Quince
If that may be, then all is well. Come, sit down every mother's son, and rehearse your parts. Pyramus, you begin. When you have spoken your speech, enter into that brake, and so everyone according to his cue.

Enter Puck

Puck
65 What hempen homespuns have we swaggering here
So near the cradle of the fairy queen?
What, a play toward? I'll be an auditor,
An actor too perhaps, if I see cause.
Quince
Speak, Pyramus! Thisbe, stand forth!
Bottom
70 [*as* Pyramus] Thisbe, the flowers of odious savours
sweet—
Quince
Odours—'odorous'!
Bottom
[*as* Pyramus]   ... odours savours sweet.
So hath thy breath, my dearest Thisbe dear.
But hark, a voice! Stay thou but here awhile,
And by and by I will to thee appear.   [*Exit*
Puck
75 A stranger Pyramus than e'er played here.   [*Exit*

77 *marry*: by the Virgin Mary.

81 *brisky juvenal*: lively young man, likely
lad.
eke: also.
Jew: The word (possibly an
abbreviation of 'jewel') is needed only
for the rhyme.

84 *Ninus*: Ninus was a king of Nineveh;
Flute's mispronunciation makes him a
'ninny' (= a fool).

90 *fair*: handsome.
were: would be.

93 *about a round*: round and about.

95–6 *Sometime . . . fire*: Puck boasted
about his skills of impersonation in
2, 1, 46–52.

96 *a fire*: a will-o'-the-wisp (= a dancing
light appearing over marshy ground,
caused by the marsh gases).

Flute
Must I speak now?
  Quince
Ay, marry must you; for you must understand he goes
but to see a noise that he heard, and is to come again.
  Flute
[*as* Thisbe] Most radiant Pyramus, most lilywhite of
  hue,
80 Of colour like the red rose on triumphant briar,
Most brisky juvenal, and eke most lovely Jew,
  As true as truest horse that yet would never tire,
I'll meet thee, Pyramus, at Ninny's tomb—
  Quince
'Ninus' tomb', man!—Why, you must not speak that yet;
85 that you answer to Pyramus. You speak all your part at
once, cues and all. Pyramus, enter—your cue is past. It
is 'never tire'.
  Flute
O—
[*as* Thisbe] As true as truest horse, that yet would
  never tire.

Enter Puck, *and* Bottom *with the ass head on*

  Bottom
90 [*as* Pyramus] If I were fair, fair Thisbe, I were only
  thine.
  Quince
O monstrous! O strange! We are haunted! Pray,
masters, fly, masters! Help!
  [*Exeunt* Quince, Snug, Flute, Snout, *and* Starveling
  Puck
I'll follow you: I'll lead you about a round,
  Through bog, through bush, through brake, through
  briar;
95 Sometime a horse I'll be, sometime a hound,
  A hog, a headless bear, sometime a fire,
And neigh, and bark, and grunt, and roar, and burn,
Like horse, hound, hog, bear, fire at every turn.   [*Exit*

99 *knavery*: trick.

Bottom

Why do they run away? This is a knavery of them to
100 make me afeard.

Enter Snout

Snout

O Bottom, thou art changed. What do I see on thee?

Bottom

What do you see? You see an ass head of your own, do
you?   [*Exit* Snou

Enter Quince

Quince

104 *translated*: transformed.

Bless thee, Bottom, bless thee! Thou art translated!
                                                   [*Ex*

Bottom

105 I see their knavery. This is to make an ass of me, to frigh
me, if they could; but I will not stir from this place, d
what they can. I will walk up and down here, and wi
108 *that*: so that.

sing, that they shall hear I am not afraid.
[*Sings*]

109 *ousel cock*: male blackbird.

   The ousel cock so black of hue,
110   With orange-tawny bill,

111 *throstle*: thrush.

   The throstle with his note so true,

112 *little quill*: shrill voice.

      The wren with little quill—

Titania

[*Waking*] What angel wakes me from my flowery bed?

Bottom

[*Sings*]
   The finch, the sparrow, and the lark,

115 *plainsong*: The cuckoo has a very
simple call—which sounds like
'cuckold' (= a man with an unfaithful
wife).

115 The plainsong cuckoo grey,
   Whose note full many a man doth mark

116–17 *Whose . . . nay*: a great many men
hear the cry and dare not deny the
charge.

      And dares not answer nay—
for indeed, who would set his wit to so foolish a bird
118 *set his wit to*: use his intelligence
against.

Who would give a bird the lie, though he cry 'cuckoo
119 *give . . . lie*: tell a bird that it is lying.
120 *never so*: ever so much.

120 never so?

Titania

122 *note*: melody.

I pray thee, gentle mortal, sing again;
Mine ear is much enamour'd of thy note.

123 *enthralled to*: enthrallèd; taken
    prisoner by.
    shape: appearance.
124 *thy fair virtue's force*: the power of
    your fine personality.
    perforce: naturally.
    move: persuade.
125 *On the first view*: at first sight.

130 *gleek*: make acute (even satiric)
    observations.

133 *to serve . . . turn*: for my purpose.

134–43 *Out . . . go*: Titania's rhyming
    couplets heighten the contrast with
    Bottom, who speaks in prose.
136 *no common rate*: no ordinary rank.
137 *still*: always.
    tend: attend.

141 *pressed*: pressèd.

So is mine eye enthralled to thy shape,
And thy fair virtue's force perforce doth move me
125 On the first view to say, to swear, I love thee.
   Bottom
Methinks, mistress, you should have little reason fo
that. And yet, to say the truth, reason and love keep littl
company together nowadays; the more the pity tha
some honest neighbours will not make them friend
130 Nay, I can gleek upon occasion.
   Titania
Thou art as wise as thou art beautiful.
   Bottom
Not so neither; but if I had wit enough to get out of th
wood, I have enough to serve mine own turn.
   Titania
Out of this wood do not desire to go:
135 Thou shalt remain here, whether thou wilt or no.
I am a spirit of no common rate;
The summer still doth tend upon my state,
And I do love thee. Therefore go with me.
I'll give thee fairies to attend on thee,
140 And they shall fetch thee jewels from the deep,
And sing, while thou on pressed flowers dost sleep;
And I will purge thy mortal grossness so
That thou shalt like an airy spirit go.
Peaseblossom, Cobweb, Moth, and Mustardseed!

   Enter four Fairies

   Peaseblossom
145 Ready.
   Cobweb
And I.
   Moth
And I.
   Mustardseed
And I.
   All
Where shall we go?

Titania

150 Be kind and courteous to this gentleman:
Hop in his walks and gambol in his eyes;
Feed him with apricocks and dewberries,
With purple grapes, green figs, and mulberries;
The honey-bags steal from the humble-bees,
155 And for night-tapers crop their waxen thighs,
And light them at the fiery glow-worms' eyes
To have my love to bed, and to arise;
And pluck the wings from painted butterflies
To fan the moonbeams from his sleeping eyes.
160 Nod to him, elves, and do him courtesies.

Peaseblossom

Hail, mortal!

Cobweb

Hail!

Moth

Hail!

Mustardseed

Hail!

Bottom

165 I cry your worships mercy, heartily. I beseech your
worship's name.

Cobweb

Cobweb.

Bottom

I shall desire you of more acquaintance, good Master
Cobweb; if I cut my finger I shall make bold with you.
170 Your name, honest gentleman?

Peaseblossom

Peaseblossom.

Bottom

I pray you commend me to Mistress Squash, your
mother, and to Master Peascod, your father. Good
Master Peaseblossom, I shall desire you of more
175 acquaintance, too.—Your name, I beseech you, sir?

Mustardseed

Mustardseed.

Bottom

Good Master Mustardseed, I know your patience well.
That same cowardly, giant-like ox-beef hath devoured

151 *in his walks*: where he walks.
gambol: romp.
in his eyes: in his sight.
152 *apricocks*: an old form of 'apricots'.
dewberries: blackberries.
154 *humble-bees*: bumble-bees.
155 *night-tapers*: candles for use at night.
crop . . . thighs: trim the wax from the bees' legs.
156 *glow-worms' eyes*: The glow-worm's light is in fact in its tail.
157 *To have*: to attend.
160 *do him courtesies*: pay him homage.

165 *I . . . mercy*: I beg your pardon.

168 *I . . . acquaintance*: the polite formula spoken when first introduced to a stranger.
169 *if . . . finger*: cobwebs (spiders' webs) were used to cover a bleeding cut.
make bold with: take advantage of.
171 *Peaseblossom*: the flower of the pea plant.
172 *Squash*: an unripe pea-pod.
173 *Peascod*: a ripe pea-pod.

176 *Mustardseed*: Mustard is used as a sharp sauce to eat with roast beef.

180 *ere*: before.

Come, wait upon him. Lead him to my bower.

183 *The moon . . . eye*: the appearance of
the moon suggests that it will rain.
184 *enforced*: enforcèd; violated.

Act 3 Scene 2
Puck boasts of his success—but Demetrius
still loves Hermia. Oberon corrects Puck's
mistake, and Demetrius declares his love
for Helena. All four lovers begin to quarrel,
but Puck is sent to distract them.

1 *be awak'd*: has woken up.

2 *eye*: sight.

3 *in extremity*: excessively.

5 *night-rule*: business of the night.

7 *close*: secret.

8 *dull*: drowsy.

9 *patches*: clowns.
rude mechanicals: rough workmen.
10 *upon . . . stalls*: in Athenian
workshops.

13 *shallowest thick-skin*: most stupid
numskull.
barren sort: dull-witted crew.
14 *Who Pyramus presented*: who played
the part of Pyramus.
15 *Forsook his scene*: left the stage.
brake: bush.
17 *nole*: headpiece.
fixed: fixèd.
18 *Anon*: presently.
answered: answerèd.
19 *mimic*: comedian.
20 *fowler*: hunter.
eye: perceive.

---

many a gentleman of your house. I promise you, your
180 kindred hath made my eyes water ere now. I desire you
of more acquaintance, good Master Mustardseed.
Titania
Come, wait upon him. Lead him to my bower.
The moon methinks looks with a watery eye,
And when she weeps, weeps every little flower
185   Lamenting some enforced chastity.
Tie up my lover's tongue; bring him silently.

[*Exeunt*

SCENE 2

Another part of the wood: enter Oberon, *King of
Fairies*

Oberon
I wonder if Titania be awak'd;
Then what it was that next came in her eye,
Which she must dote on, in extremity.

Enter Puck

Here comes my messenger. How now, mad spirit?
5 What night-rule now about this haunted grove?
Puck
My mistress with a monster is in love.
Near to her close and consecrated bower,
While she was in her dull and sleeping hour,
A crew of patches, rude mechanicals,
10 That work for bread upon Athenian stalls,
Were met together to rehearse a play
Intended for great Theseus' nuptial day.
The shallowest thick-skin of that barren sort,
Who Pyramus presented, in their sport
15 Forsook his scene and enter'd in a brake,
When I did him at this advantage take:
An ass's nole I fixed on his head.
Anon his Thisbe must be answered,
And forth my mimic comes. When they him spy—
20 As wild geese that the creeping fowler eye,

21 *russet-pated . . . sort*: a large flock of grey-headed jackdaws.

23 *Sever*: separate.
24 *at his sight*: at the sight of him.
25 *at our stamp*: when I stamped on the ground.
26 *He*: one man.
27 *lost with*: conquered by.
28 *senseless things*: inanimate objects. *wrong*: injury.

30 *from . . . catch*: everything catches at those who run away in fear.

32 *translated*: transformed.

36 *latch'd*: captured.

38 *took*: caught.

40 *of force . . . ey'd*: he would be forced to see her.

41 *close*: hidden.

44 *Lay . . . bitter*: use such cruel language.

48 *Being . . . blood*: having waded so far in blood.

Or russet-pated choughs, many in sort,
Rising and cawing at the gun's report,
Sever themselves and madly sweep the sky—
So at his sight away his fellows fly,
25 And at our stamp here o'er and o'er one falls;
He 'Murder!' cries, and help from Athens calls.
Their sense thus weak, lost with their fears thus strong,
Made senseless things begin to do them wrong,
For briars and thorns at their apparel snatch,
30 Some sleeves, some hats; from yielders all things catch.
I led them on in this distracted fear,
And left sweet Pyramus translated there;
When in that moment, so it came to pass,
Titania wak'd, and straightway loved an ass.
Oberon
35 This falls out better than I could devise.
But hast thou yet latch'd the Athenian's eyes
With the love juice, as I did bid thee do?
Puck
I took him sleeping—that is finished too—
And the Athenian woman by his side,
40 That when he wak'd, of force she must be ey'd.

Enter Demetrius *and* Hermia

Oberon
Stand close: this is the same Athenian.
Puck
This is the woman, but not this the man.
Demetrius
O, why rebuke you him that loves you so?
Lay breath so bitter on your bitter foe.
Hermia
45 Now I but chide; but I should use thee worse,
For thou, I fear, hast given me cause to curse.
If thou hast slain Lysander in his sleep,
Being o'er shoes in blood, plunge in the deep,
And kill me too.
50 The sun was not so true unto the day
As he to me. Would he have stol'n away
From sleeping Hermia? I'll believe as soon

This whole earth may be bor'd, and that the moon
May through the centre creep, and so displease
55 Her brother's noontide with th'Antipodes.
It cannot be but thou hast murder'd him:
So should a murderer look; so dead, so grim.
    Demetrius
So should the murder'd look, and so should I,
Pierc'd through the heart with your stern cruelty;
60 Yet you, the murderer, look as bright, as clear,
As yonder Venus in her glimmering sphere.
    Hermia
What's this to my Lysander? Where is he?
Ah, good Demetrius, wilt thou give him me?
    Demetrius
I had rather give his carcass to my hounds.
    Hermia
65 Out, dog! Out, cur! Thou driv'st me past the bounds
Of maiden's patience. Hast thou slain him then?
Henceforth be never number'd among men.
O, once tell true; tell true, even for my sake:
Durst thou have look'd upon him being awake?
70 And hast thou kill'd him sleeping? O, brave touch!
Could not a worm, an adder do so much?
An adder did it; for with doubler tongue
Than thine, thou serpent, never adder stung.
    Demetrius
You spend your passion on a mispris'd mood.
75 I am not guilty of Lysander's blood,
Nor is he dead, for aught that I can tell.
    Hermia
I pray thee, tell me then that he is well.
    Demetrius
And if I could, what should I get therefor?
    Hermia
A privilege, never to see me more;
80 And from thy hated presence part I so.
See me no more, whether he be dead or no.   [*Exit*
    Demetrius
There is no following her in this fierce vein;
Here therefore for a while I will remain.

84–5 *So . . . owe*: the burden of sorrow grows heavier through lack of sleep, due to sorrow.

86–7 *Which . . . stay*: sleep is going to pay back a little of what I am missing if I can accept the offer ('tender') of some sleep now.

88 *quite*: completely.

89 *true love*: true lover.

90 *misprision*: mistake.

91 *true love turn'd*: true love turned false.

92–3 *Then . . . oath*: that's because fate has ordained that, for every man who keeps his word, a million fail, breaking one promise after another.

96 *fancy-sick*: love-sick.
cheer: complexion.

97 *costs . . . dear*: Elizabethans thought that every sigh dried up a drop of blood.

98 *illusion*: trick.

99 *against . . . appear*: in preparation for when she comes.

101 *Tartar's bow*: The fierce Tartars (from central Asia) fought with curved (lip-shaped) bows and arrows.

102 *dye*: colour.

104 *apple*: pupil.

108 *by*: near.

So sorrow's heaviness doth heavier grow
85 For debt that bankrupt sleep doth sorrow owe,
Which now in some slight measure it will pay,
If for his tender here I make some stay.

He lies down and sleeps

Oberon
What hast thou done? Thou hast mistaken quite,
And laid the love juice on some true love's sight.
90 Of thy misprision must perforce ensue
Some true love turn'd, and not a false turn'd true.
    Puck
Then fate o'errules, that, one man holding troth,
A million fail, confounding oath on oath.
    Oberon
About the wood go swifter than the wind,
95 And Helena of Athens look thou find.
All fancy-sick she is and pale of cheer
With sighs of love, that costs the fresh blood dear.
By some illusion see thou bring her here;
I'll charm his eyes against she do appear.
    Puck
100 I go, I go, look how I go!
Swifter than arrow from the Tartar's bow.   [*Exit*
    Oberon
    [*Squeezing the juice on* Demetrius's *eyes*]
    Flower of this purple dye,
    Hit with Cupid's archery,
    Sink in apple of his eye.
105 When his love he doth espy,
    Let her shine as gloriously
    As the Venus of the sky.
    When thou wak'st, if she be by,
    Beg of her for remedy.

Enter Puck

Puck
110   Captain of our fairy band,
Helena is here at hand,
And the youth mistook by me,
Pleading for a lover's fee.
Shall we their fond pageant see?
115   Lord, what fools these mortals be!
Oberon
Stand aside. The noise they make
Will cause Demetrius to awake.
Puck
Then will two at once woo one—
That must needs be sport alone;
120   And those things do best please me
That befall prepost'rously.

Enter Lysander *and* Helena

Lysander
Why should you think that I should woo in scorn?
   Scorn and derision never come in tears.
Look when I vow, I weep; and vows so born,
125   In their nativity all truth appears.
How can these things in me seem scorn to you,
Bearing the badge of faith to prove them true?
   Helena
You do advance your cunning more and more.
   When truth kills truth, O devilish-holy fray!
130   These vows are Hermia's. Will you give her o'er?
   Weigh oath with oath, and you will nothing weigh;
Your vows to her and me, put in two scales,
Will even weigh, and both as light as tales.
   Lysander
I had no judgement when to her I swore.
   Helena
135   Nor none, in my mind, now you give her o'er.
   Lysander
Demetrius loves her, and he loves not you.

113 *lover's fee*: i.e. to be loved in return.
114 *fond pageant*: foolish exhibition of themselves.

118 *at once*: at the same time.
119 *That . . . alone*: that will be funny enough in itself.
121 *befall*: happen.
prepost'rously: extraordinarily.

124–5 *vows . . . appears*: vows which are born in weeping show from their birth that they are genuine.
126–7 *How . . . true*: how can you scorn my protestations of love when they have the badges of truth (i.e. his tears).
128 *advance*: display.
129 *truth kills truth*: one true love kills another.
devilish-holy fray: damnable holy war.
130 *give her o'er*: renounce your love for her.
131 *nothing weigh*: cancel each other out; have no weight (because they are both false).

133 *tales*: fictions, falsehoods.

Demetrius

[*Waking*] O Helen, goddess, nymph, perfect, divine!
To what, my love, shall I compare thine eyne?
Crystal is muddy! O, how ripe in show
140 Thy lips, those kissing cherries, tempting grow!
That pure congealed white, high Taurus' snow,
Fann'd with the eastern wind, turns to a crow
When thou hold'st up thy hand. O, let me kiss
This princess of pure white, this seal of bliss!

Helena

145 O spite! O Hell! I see you all are bent
To set against me for your merriment.
If you were civil, and knew courtesy,
You would not do me thus much injury.
Can you not hate me, as I know you do,
150 But you must join in souls to mock me too?
If you were men, as men you are in show,
You would not use a gentle lady so,
To vow, and swear, and superpraise my parts,
When I am sure you hate me with your hearts.
155 You both are rivals, and love Hermia;
And now both rivals to mock Helena.
A trim exploit, a manly enterprise,
To conjure tears up in a poor maid's eyes
With your derision! None of noble sort
160 Would so offend a virgin, and extort
A poor soul's patience, all to make you sport.

Lysander

You are unkind, Demetrius: be not so,
For you love Hermia—this you know I know—
And here with all good will, with all my heart,
165 In Hermia's love I yield you up my part;
And yours of Helena to me bequeath,
Whom I do love, and will do till my death.

Helena

Never did mockers waste more idle breath.

Demetrius

Lysander, keep thy Hermia; I will none.
170 If e'er I lov'd her, all that love is gone.
My heart to her but as guest-wise sojourn'd,

138 *eyne*: eyes.

141 *congealed*: congealèd.
Taurus: a mountain range in Turkey.

143 *When . . . hand*: Helena has perhaps
held up her hands in despair, or to
push Demetrius away from her.
144 *princess . . . white*: sovereign
whiteness.
seal of bliss: To take Helena's hand
(as in marriage) would make
Demetrius's happiness complete.
145 *bent*: determined.
146 *set against*: attack.

150 *in souls*: in heart and soul, with all
your beings.
151 *show*: appearance.

153 *superpraise*: praise with superlatives.

157 *trim*: fine.

159 *sort*: birth.
160 *extort*: torment.

166 *bequeath*: assign, make over.

169 *I will none*: I will have nothing to do
with her.

171 *My heart . . . sojourn'd*: my heart was
only visiting her as a guest.

And now to Helen is it home return'd,
There to remain.
Lysander
                    Helen, it is not so.
Demetrius
Disparage not the faith thou dost not know,
175 Lest to thy peril thou aby it dear.
Look where thy love comes: yonder is thy dear.

Enter Hermia

Hermia
Dark night, that from the eye his function takes,
The ear more quick of apprehension makes;
Wherein it doth impair the seeing sense
180 It pays the hearing double recompense.
Thou art not by mine eye, Lysander, found;
Mine ear, I thank it, brought me to thy sound.
But why unkindly didst thou leave me so?
Lysander
Why should he stay whom love doth press to go?
Hermia
185 What love could press Lysander from my side?
Lysander
Lysander's love, that would not let him bide,
Fair Helena—who more engilds the night
Than all yon fiery oes and eyes of light.
[*To* Hermia] Why seek'st thou me? Could not this
    make thee know
190 The hate I bare thee made me leave thee so?
Hermia
You speak not as you think; it cannot be.
Helena
Lo, she is one of this confederacy!
Now I perceive they have conjoin'd all three
To fashion this false sport in spite of me.
195 Injurious Hermia, most ungrateful maid,
Have you conspir'd, have you with these contriv'd
To bait me with this foul derision?

---

175 *aby it dear*: pay dearly for it.

177–8 *from . . . makes*: takes sight from the eye and makes the hearing more acute.
179–80 *Wherein . . . recompense*: where it damages the sight, it gives double compensation to the hearing.
182 *thy sound*: the sound of your voice.

184 *press*: urge.

186 *bide*: stay.
187 *engilds*: lights up.
188 *yon . . . light*: the stars; 'oes' were glittering spangles used for dress decoration.
190 *bare*: felt towards.
193 *conjoin'd*: joined together.
194 *in spite of*: in scorn of.
195 *Injurious*: insulting; Helena speaks now in blank verse (instead of rhyming couplets) as the quarrel grows serious.
196 *contriv'd*: plotted.
197 *bait*: Helena is comparing herself with a bear, which was tormented ('baited') by dogs in so-called 'sport'.

Is all the counsel that we two have shar'd,
The sisters' vows, the hours that we have spent
200 When we have chid the hasty-footed time
For parting us—O, is all forgot?
All schooldays' friendship, childhood innocence?
We, Hermia, like two artificial gods
Have with our needles created both one flower,
205 Both on one sampler, sitting on one cushion,
Both warbling of one song, both in one key,
As if our hands, our sides, voices, and minds
Had been incorporate. So we grew together
Like to a double cherry, seeming parted,
210 But yet an union in partition,
Two lovely berries moulded on one stem;
So with two seeming bodies but one heart,
Two of the first, like coats in heraldry,
Due but to one, and crowned with one crest.
215 And will you rent our ancient love asunder,
To join with men in scorning your poor friend?
It is not friendly, 'tis not maidenly.
Our sex, as well as I, may chide you for it,
Though I alone do feel the injury.

Hermia

220 I am amazed at your passionate words.
I scorn you not; it seems that you scorn me.

Helena

Have you not set Lysander, as in scorn,
To follow me, and praise my eyes and face?
And made your other love, Demetrius,
225 Who even but now did spurn me with his foot,
To call me goddess, nymph, divine and rare,
Precious, celestial? Wherefore speaks he this
To her he hates? And wherefore doth Lysander
Deny your love, so rich within his soul,
230 And tender me, forsooth, affection,
But by your setting on, by your consent?
What though I be not so in grace as you,
So hung upon with love, so fortunate,
But miserable most, to love unlov'd:
235 This you should pity rather than despise.

200 *chid*: reproached.

203 *artificial gods*: gods with skill in creative art.
204 *needle*: The word is pronounced here as one syllable—'neele'.
205 *sampler*: piece of embroidery.
206 *in one key*: i.e. in perfect harmony.

208 *incorporate*: of a single body.

210 *partition*: separation.

212 *with . . . heart*: apparently with two bodies, but with one heart.
213–14 *Two . . . crest*: two equal halves of a shield, both of the same background colour ('the first'), belonging ('Due') to only one person and surmounted with a single crest; the heraldic sense of 'partition' has led Helena to this metaphor. Shakespeare was granted his own coat-of-arms shortly after writing this play.

214 *crowned*: crownèd.
215 *rent . . . asunder*: tear our former love apart.
220 *amazed*: amazèd.
225 *even but now*: very recently.
229 *your love*: his love for you.
230 *tender*: offer.
forsooth: indeed.
232 *grace*: favour.

Hermia
I understand not what you mean by this.
   Helena
Ay, do! Persever, counterfeit sad looks,
Make mouths upon me when I turn my back,
Wink each at other, hold the sweet jest up.
240 This sport, well carried, shall be chronicled.
If you have any pity, grace, or manners,
You would not make me such an argument.
But fare ye well. 'Tis partly my own fault,
Which death or absence soon shall remedy.
   Lysander
245 Stay, gentle Helena: hear my excuse,
My love, my life, my soul, fair Helena!
   Helena
O, excellent!
   Hermia
[*To* Lysander] Sweet, do not scorn her so.
   Demetrius
If she cannot entreat, I can compel.
   Lysander
Thou canst compel no more than she entreat;
250 Thy threats have no more strength than her weak
     prayers.
Helen, I love thee, by my life, I do:
I swear by that which I will lose for thee
To prove him false that says I love thee not.
   Demetrius
I say I love thee more than he can do.
   Lysander
255 If thou say so, withdraw, and prove it too.
   Demetrius
Quick, come.
   Hermia
              Lysander, whereto tends all this?
   Lysander
Away, you Ethiop!
   Demetrius
              No, no, sir,
Seem to break loose, take on as you would follow,
But yet come not. You are a tame man, go.

---

237 *Persever*: persevere, carry on; the word here is stressed on the first syllable. *sad looks*: solemn faces.
239 *hold . . . up*: keep up this fine joke.

242 *argument*: subject of dispute.

255 *withdraw*: move away. *prove it*: i.e. by fighting a duel.

257 *Ethiop*: blackamoor; Lysander intends to insult Hermia because of her dark complexion (which was unfashionable in Elizabethan England).
258 *take on*: pretend.
259 *tame*: spiritless.

260 *burr*: the prickly seed-head of a thistle (which is impossible to shake off).

Lysander
260 Hang off, thou cat, thou burr! Vile thing, let loose,
Or I will shake thee from me like a serpent.

Hermia
Why are you grown so rude? What change is this,
Sweet love?

Lysander
            Thy love?—out, tawny Tartar, out;
Out, loath'd medicine! O hated potion, hence!

264 *tawny Tartar*: dusky warrior (see 101note).

Hermia
265 Do you not jest?

Helena
            Yes, sooth, and so do you.

Lysander
Demetrius, I will keep my word with thee.

Demetrius
I would I had your bond, for I perceive
A weak bond holds you. I'll not trust your word.

267 *bond*: contract; means of restraint.
268 *weak bond*: i.e. Hermia's arms.

Lysander
What? Should I hurt her, strike her, kill her dead?
270 Although I hate her, I'll not harm her so.

Hermia
What? Can you do me greater harm than hate?
Hate me? Wherefore? O me, what news, my love?
Am not I Hermia? Are not you Lysander?
I am as fair now as I was erewhile.
275 Since night you loved me; yet since night you left me.
Why then, you left me—O, the gods forbid!—
In earnest, shall I say?

272 *what news*: what's going on.

274 *erewhile*: a short time ago.

275 *Since night*: since night fell.

277 *In earnest*: seriously, not as a joke.

Lysander
            Ay, by my life;
And never did desire to see thee more.
Therefore be out of hope, of question, of doubt;
280 Be certain, nothing truer—'tis no jest
That I do hate thee and love Helena.

Hermia
[*To* Helena] O me, you juggler, you canker-blossom,
You thief of love! What, have you come by night
And stol'n my love's heart from him?

282 *juggler*: trickster.
canker-blossom: worm-eaten flower.

Helena
            Fine, i'faith!

284 *Fine, i'faith!*: Helena persists in believing that there is a conspiracy against her.

286–343 *What . . . away*: The two girls
quarrel about their difference in
colouring, in height, and in
temperament.

288 *counterfeit*: cheat.

290 *compare*: comparison.

291 *urg'd*: boasted about.

296 *painted*: i.e. with cosmetics (generally
disapproved of by the Elizabethans).
maypole: a tall pole erected on the
village green for the traditional May
dancing.

300 *curst*: bad-tempered.

301 *shrewishness*: quarrelling.

302 *right*: true.

308 *counsels*: secrets.

310 *stealth*: stealing away.

312 *chid me hence*: ordered me to go away
from here.

314 *so*: provided that.
quiet: peacefully.

317 *fond*: foolish.

285 Have you no modesty, no maiden shame,
No touch of bashfulness? What, will you tear
Impatient answers from my gentle tongue?
Fie, fie, you counterfeit, you puppet, you!

Hermia
'Puppet'? Why so?—Ay, that way goes the game.
290 Now I perceive that she hath made compare
Between our statures; she hath urg'd her height,
And with her personage, her tall personage,
Her height, forsooth, she hath prevail'd with him.
And are you grown so high in his esteem
295 Because I am so dwarfish and so low?
How low am I, thou painted maypole? Speak!
How low am I? I am not yet so low
But that my nails can reach unto thine eyes.

Helena
I pray you, though you mock me, gentlemen,
300 Let her not hurt me. I was never curst;
I have no gift at all in shrewishness.
I am a right maid for my cowardice;
Let her not strike me. You perhaps may think
Because she is something lower than myself
305 That I can match her.

Hermia
                              Lower? Hark, again!

Helena
Good Hermia, do not be so bitter with me.
I evermore did love you, Hermia,
Did ever keep your counsels, never wrong'd you,
Save that in love unto Demetrius
310 I told him of your stealth unto this wood.
He follow'd you; for love I follow'd him,
But he hath chid me hence, and threaten'd me
To strike me, spurn me, nay, to kill me too.
And now, so you will let me quiet go,
315 To Athens will I bear my folly back,
And follow you no further. Let me go;
You see how simple and how fond I am.

Hermia
Why, get you gone! Who is't that hinders you?

Helena
A foolish heart that I leave here behind.
    Hermia
320 What, with Lysander?
    Helena
                         With Demetrius.
    Lysander
Be not afraid; she shall not harm thee, Helena.
    Demetrius
No, sir. She shall not, though you take her part.
    Helena
O, when she is angry she is keen and shrewd;
She was a vixen when she went to school,
325 And though she be but little, she is fierce.
    Hermia
Little again! Nothing but low and little?
Why will you suffer her to flout me thus?
Let me come to her.
    Lysander
                    Get you gone, you dwarf,
You minimus of hindering knot-grass made,
330 You bead, you acorn.
    Demetrius
                     You are too officious
In her behalf that scorns your services.
Let her alone: speak not of Helena,
Take not her part; for if thou dost intend
Never so little show of love to her,
335 Thou shalt aby it.
    Lysander
               Now she holds me not—
Now follow, if thou dur'st, to try whose right,
Of thine or mine, is most in Helena.
    Demetrius
Follow? Nay, I'll go with thee, cheek by jowl.
                 [*Exeunt* Lysander *and* Demetrius
    Hermia
You, mistress, all this coil is 'long of you.
340 Nay, go not back.

---

323 *keen and shrewd*: cruel and malicious.
324 *vixen*: The female fox is even more savage than the male.

325 *but*: only.
327 *flout*: mock.
329 *minimus*: insignificant little creature (a Shakespearean coinage).
    knot-grass: a low-growing weed with creeping stems.
330 *officious*: interfering.
333–4 *if . . . her*: if you pretend to show the least sign of love for her.
335 *aby it*: pay for it.
336 *try*: make trial (in a duel).

338 *cheek by jowl*: side by side.

339 *coil*: trouble.
    'long of: on account of.

Helena

I will not trust you, I,
Nor longer stay in your curst company.
Your hands than mine are quicker for a fray;
My legs are longer, though, to run away!   [*Exit*

Hermia

I am amaz'd, and know not what to say.   [*Exit*

Oberon *and* Puck *come forward*

Oberon

345 This is thy negligence. Still thou mistak'st,
Or else committ'st thy knaveries wilfully.

Puck

Believe me, King of Shadows, I mistook.
Did not you tell me I should know the man
By the Athenian garments he had on?
350 And so far blameless proves my enterprise
That I have 'nointed an Athenian's eyes;
And so far am I glad it so did sort,
As this their jangling I esteem a sport.

Oberon

Thou seest these lovers seek a place to fight:
355 Hie therefore, Robin, overcast the night;
The starry welkin cover thou anon
With drooping fog as black as Acheron,
And lead these testy rivals so astray
As one come not within another's way.
360 Like to Lysander sometime frame thy tongue,
Then stir Demetrius up with bitter wrong,
And sometime rail thou like Demetrius;
And from each other look thou lead them thus,
Till o'er their brows death-counterfeiting sleep
365 With leaden legs and batty wings doth creep.
Then crush this herb into Lysander's eye,
Whose liquor hath this virtuous property,
To take from thence all error with his might,
And make his eyeballs roll with wonted sight.
370 When they next wake, all this derision
Shall seem a dream and fruitless vision,

---

345 *still thou mistak'st*: you are always making mistakes.

352 *sort*: turn out.
353 *jangling*: quarrelling.
     esteem a sport: consider a joke.

356 *welkin*: sky.
     anon: at once.
357 *Acheron*: a black river in the classical underworld.
358 *testy*: irritable.
360 *frame thy tongue*: make your voice sound.
361 *stir . . . wrong*: provoke Demetrius with unjust accusations.
362 *rail*: insult.
364 *death-counterfeiting sleep*: sleep that looks like death.
365 *batty*: bat-like (i.e. silent).

367 *virtuous property*: healing power.

370 *derision*: delusion.
371 *fruitless*: meaningless.

372 *wend*: return.
373 *league*: union.
whose . . . end: which will last as long
    as they live.
375 *I'll to*: I'll go to.
376 *charmed*: charmèd.

379 *dragons*: The chariot of the goddess of
    the night was drawn across the sky by
    dragons.
    full: very.
380 *Aurora's harbinger*: the morning star
    (Phosphor) which heralds the
    approach of dawn (the goddess
    Aurora).
382–4 *Damned . . . gone*: damnèd; the
    ghosts of those who have committed
    suicide (and been damned for this)
    have already gone to the crossroads
    (where suicides were buried) or back
    into the waters where they drowned
    themselves.
389 *I . . . sport*: Perhaps Oberon is
    boasting that he has made love to
    Aurora, goddess of dawn; or he may
    refer to hunting with Cephalus,
    beloved of Aurora.
390 *forester*: gamekeeper.
392 *Neptune*: god of the ocean.
    blessed: blessèd.
395 *effect*: complete.

399 *Goblin*: hobgoblin—i.e. Puck himself;
    see *2*, 1, 40.

402 *drawn*: with sword drawn.

403 *straight*: straightaway, immediately.

And back to Athens shall the lovers wend
With league whose date till death shall never end.
Whiles I in this affair do thee employ
375 I'll to my queen and beg her Indian boy;
And then I will her charmed eye release
From monster's view, and all things shall be peace.
   Puck
My fairy lord, this must be done with haste,
For night's swift dragons cut the clouds full fast,
380 And yonder shines Aurora's harbinger,
At whose approach ghosts wandering here and there
Troop home to churchyards. Damned spirits all,
That in crossways and floods have burial,
Already to their wormy beds are gone.
385 For fear lest day should look their shames upon,
They wilfully themselves exile from light,
And must for aye consort with black-brow'd night.
   Oberon
But we are spirits of another sort.
I with the morning's love have oft made sport,
390 And like a forester the groves may tread
Even till the eastern gate, all fiery-red,
Opening on Neptune with fair blessed beams,
Turns into yellow gold his salt green streams.
But notwithstanding, haste, make no delay;
395 We may effect this business yet ere day.   [*Exit*
   Puck
Up and down, up and down,
I will lead them up and down;
I am fear'd in field and town.
Goblin, lead them up and down.
400 Here comes one.

   Enter Lysander

   Lysander
Where art thou, proud Demetrius? Speak thou now.
   Puck
Here, villain, drawn and ready! Where art thou?
   Lysander
I will be with thee straight.

Puck

                                        Follow me then
To plainer ground.   [*Exit* Lysander

Enter Demetrius

Demetrius

                              Lysander, speak again.
405 Thou runaway, thou coward, art thou fled?
Speak! In some bush? Where dost thou hide thy head?
      Puck
Thou coward, art thou bragging to the stars,
Telling the bushes that thou look'st for wars,
And wilt not come? Come, recreant, come, thou child,
410 I'll whip thee with a rod. He is defil'd
That draws a sword on thee.
      Demetrius
                              Yea, art thou there?
      Puck
Follow my voice. We'll try no manhood here.
                                        [*Exeunt*

Enter Lysander

Lysander
He goes before me, and still dares me on;
When I come where he calls, then he is gone.
415 The villain is much lighter-heel'd than I;
I follow'd fast, but faster he did fly,
That fallen am I in dark uneven way,
And here will rest me. [*Lies down*] Come, thou gentle
      day,
For if but once thou show me thy grey light
420 I'll find Demetrius and revenge this spite. [*Sleeps*]

404 *plainer*: more open.

407 *bragging*: boasting.

409 *recreant*: coward.
410 *defil'd*: dishonoured.

412 *try no manhood*: make no test of courage.

413 *still*: always.
dares me on: challenges me to follow.
414 *where*: to where.

417 *That*: with the result that.
in: into.

Enter Puck *and* Demetrius

Puck
Ho, ho, ho! Coward, why com'st thou not?
Demetrius
Abide me if thou dar'st, for well I wot
Thou runn'st before me, shifting every place,
And dar'st not stand nor look me in the face.
425 Where art thou now?
Puck
                              Come hither; I am here.
Demetrius
Nay then, thou mock'st me. Thou shalt buy this dear
If ever I thy face by daylight see.
Now, go thy way; faintness constraineth me
To measure out my length on this cold bed.
430 By day's approach look to be visited. [*Sleeps*]

Enter Helena

Helena
O weary night, O long and tedious night,
    Abate thy hours, shine comforts from the east,
That I may back to Athens by daylight
    From these that my poor company detest;
435 And sleep, that sometimes shuts up sorrow's eye,
Steal me awhile from mine own company. [*Sleeps*]
Puck
Yet but three? Come one more,
Two of both kinds makes up four.
Here she comes, curst and sad.
440 Cupid is a knavish lad
Thus to make poor females mad.

422 *Abide me*: wait for me.
wot: know.
423 *shifting . . . place*: always changing places.

426 *buy this dear*: pay dearly for this.

429 *measure . . . length*: stretch myself out.
430 *visited*: found out.

432 *Abate*: shorten.

434 *my poor company*: the company of poor me.

439 *curst*: cross.

Enter Hermia

Hermia
Never so weary, never so in woe,
  Bedabbled with the dew, and torn with briars—
I can no further crawl, no further go;
445   My legs can keep no pace with my desires.
Here will I rest me till the break of day.
Heavens shield Lysander, if they mean a fray. [*Sleeps*]
  Puck
    On the ground
    Sleep sound.
450   I'll apply
    To your eye,
  Gentle lover, remedy.

Squeezes the juice on Lysander's *eyes*

    When thou wak'st,
    Thou tak'st
455   True delight
    In the sight
    Of thy former lady's eye;
    And the country proverb known,
    That every man should take his own,
460   In your waking shall be shown.
      Jack shall have Jill,
      Naught shall go ill:
  The man shall have his mare again, and all shall be
    well.
            [*Exit* Puck; *the lovers remain on stage, asleep*

444 *go*: walk.

447 *mean a fray*: intend to fight.

461–3 *Jack . . . again*: Puck combines two proverbial sayings: 'All shall be well, and Jack shall have Jill', 'All is well, and the man has his mare again'.

ACT 4

SCENE 1

The wood: enter Titania, *Queen of Fairies, and*
Bottom, *and* Fairies *including* Peaseblossom,
Cobweb, *and* Mustardseed; *and the King* Oberon
behind them

Titania
Come, sit thee down upon this flowery bed
  While I thy amiable cheeks do coy,
And stick musk-roses in thy sleek smooth head,
  And kiss thy fair large ears, my gentle joy.
Bottom
5 Where's Peaseblossom?
Peaseblossom
Ready.
Bottom
Scratch my head, Peaseblossom. Where's Mounsieur
Cobweb?
Cobweb
Ready.
Bottom
10 Mounsieur Cobweb, good Mounsieur, get you your
weapons in your hand, and kill me a red-hipped
humble-bee on the top of a thistle; and, good
Mounsieur, bring me the honey-bag. Do not fret
yourself too much in the action, Mounsieur; and, good
15 Mounsieur, have a care the honey-bag break not; I
would be loath to have you overflown with a honey-
bag, signior. Where's Mounsieur Mustardseed?
Mustardseed
Ready.
Bottom
Give me your neaf, Mounsieur Mustardseed. Pray you,
20 leave your courtesy, good Mounsieur.

2 *amiable*: loveable.
  coy: caress.

7 *Mounsieur*: Monsieur: Bottom
addresses the fairies as though they
were French or Italian gentlemen.

13 *fret*: trouble.

16 *be loath*: hate.
  overflown: swamped.
17 *signior*: signor, sir.
19 *neaf*: hand.
20 *leave your courtesy*: stop bowing to
me; Bottom wants to shake hands
with the fairy, who insists on showing
the respect that Titania commanded
(*3, 1, 150*).

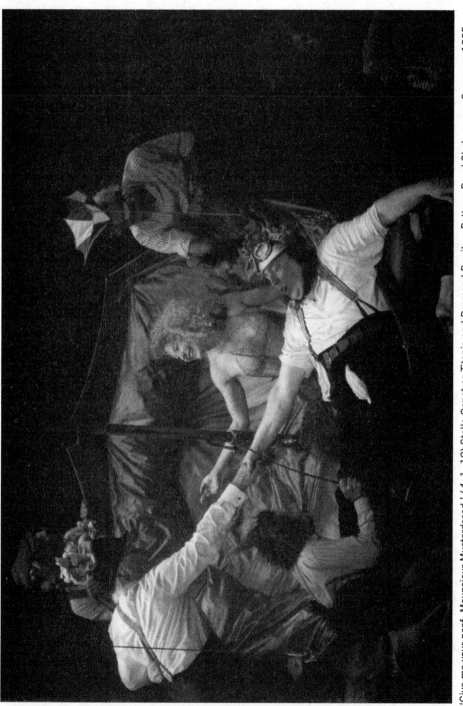

'Give me your neaf, Mounsieur Mustardseed.' (4, 1, 19) Stella Gonet as Titania and Desmond Barrit as Bottom, Royal Shakespeare Company, 1995.

Mustardseed

What's your will?

Bottom

Nothing, good Mounsieur, but to help Cavalery
Peaseblossom to scratch. I must to the barber's,
Mounsieur, for methinks I am marvellous hairy about
25 the face. And I am such a tender ass, if my hair do but
tickle me, I must scratch.

Titania

What, wilt thou hear some music, my sweet love?

Bottom

I have a reasonable good ear in music. Let's have the
tongs and the bones.

Titania

30 Or say, sweet love, what thou desir'st to eat.

Bottom

Truly, a peck of provender, I could munch your good
dry oats. Methinks I have a great desire to a bottle of
hay. Good hay, sweet hay hath no fellow.

Titania

I have a venturous fairy that shall seek
35 The squirrel's hoard, and fetch thee new nuts.

Bottom

I had rather have a handful or two of dried peas. But, I
pray you, let none of your people stir me; I have an
exposition of sleep come upon me.

Titania

Sleep thou, and I will wind thee in my arms.
40 Fairies be gone, and be all ways away.

[*Exeunt* Fairies

So doth the woodbine the sweet honeysuckle
Gently entwist; the female ivy so
Enrings the barky fingers of the elm.
O, how I love thee! How I dote on thee! [*They sleep*]

Enter Puck

Oberon

45 [*Coming forward*] Welcome, good Robin. Seest thou
this sweet sight?

---

22 *Cavalery*: cavaliere.

24 *marvellous*: unusually.
25 *ass*: fool (with obvious irony).

29 *the . . . bones*: metal tongs struck
with a key, and bone clappers rattled
between the fingers.

31 *peck*: bundle (literally, a quarter of a
bushel).
provender: fodder.
32 *bottle*: truss, small bundle.
33 *fellow*: equal.

37 *stir*: disturb.
38 *exposition of*: Bottom means
'disposition to'.

39 *wind*: wrap.
40 *all ways*: in all directions.

41 *woodbine*: bindweed or convulvulus.
42 *The female ivy*: Proverbially the vine
(= wife) embraces the elm
(= husband).
43 *barky fingers*: branches covered with
bark.

46 *dotage*: obsession.
47 *of late*: recently.
48 *favours*: gifts of flowers.
49 *upbraid*: reproach.
50 *rounded*: encircled.

52 *sometime*: formerly.
53 *orient*: lustrous.
54 *flowerets*: little flowers.

57 *mild terms*: gentle language.
58 *ask of her*: ask her to give me.
59 *straight*: immediately.

63 *transformed*: transformèd.

65 *other*: others.
66 *repair*: return.
67 *accidents*: happenings.
68 *fierce*: extravagant.

70 *wont*: accustomed.

72 *Dian's bud*: Oberon explained
(*2*, 1, 184) that he can remove this
spell with 'another herb'—perhaps
artemisia (wormwood), a plant sacred
to Artemis (Diana) goddess of chastity.
Cupid's flower: see *2*, 1, 155–68.
73 *blessed*: blessèd.
76 *enamour'd of*: in love with.

77 *pass*: happen.

Her dotage now I do begin to pity;
For, meeting her of late behind the wood
Seeking sweet favours for this hateful fool,
I did upbraid her and fall out with her,
50 For she his hairy temples then had rounded
With coronet of fresh and fragrant flowers;
And that same dew, which sometime on the buds
Was wont to swell like round and orient pearls,
Stood now within the pretty flowerets' eyes
55 Like tears that did their own disgrace bewail.
When I had at my pleasure taunted her,
And she in mild terms begg'd my patience,
I then did ask of her her changeling child,
Which straight she gave me, and her fairy sent
60 To bear him to my bower in Fairyland.
And now I have the boy, I will undo
This hateful imperfection of her eyes.
And, gentle Puck, take this transformed scalp
From off the head of this Athenian swain,
65 That, he awaking when the other do,
May all to Athens back again repair,
And think no more of this night's accidents
But as the fierce vexation of a dream.
But first I will release the fairy queen. [*Squeezing a herb
on* Titania's *eyes*]
70   Be as thou wast wont to be;
        See as thou wast wont to see.
        Dian's bud o'er Cupid's flower
        Hath such force and blessed power.
Now, my Titania, wake you, my sweet queen!
        Titania
75 [*Starting up*] My Oberon, what visions have I seen!
Methought I was enamour'd of an ass.
        Oberon
There lies your love.
        Titania
                            How came these things to pass?
O, how mine eyes do loathe his visage now!
        Oberon
Silence awhile: Robin, take off this head.

80–1 *strike . . . sense*: charm the senses of all these five into an abnormally deep sleep.

80 Titania, music call, and strike more dead
Than common sleep of all these five the sense.
Titania
Music, ho, music such as charmeth sleep!

Soft music plays

Puck
[*To* Bottom, *removing the ass's head*] Now when thou
wak'st, with thine own fool's eyes peep.
Oberon

84–5 *take hands . . . be*: The dance marks the renewal of love and harmony between Oberon and Titania.

Sound, music! Come, my queen, take hands with me,
85 And rock the ground whereon these sleepers be.

They dance

86 *amity*: friendship.
87 *solemnly*: ceremoniously.

Now thou and I are new in amity,
And will tomorrow midnight solemnly
Dance in Duke Theseus' house triumphantly,

89 *to*: with.

And bless it to all fair prosperity.
90 There shall the pairs of faithful lovers be
Wedded, with Theseus, all in jollity.
Puck
Fairy king, attend, and mark:
I do hear the morning lark.
Oberon

94 *sad*: sober.

Then, my queen, in silence sad,
95 Trip we after night's shade;

96 *compass*: encompass.

We the globe can compass soon,
Swifter than the wandering moon.
Titania
Come, my lord, and in our flight
Tell me how it came this night
100 That I sleeping here was found
With these mortals on the ground.
[*Exeunt* Oberon, Titania, *and* Puck

101s.d. *Wind*: blow; the offstage hunting-horns announce the coming of day.

103 *observation*: ritual (to celebrate May Day).

104 *the vaward*: the first part.

105 *music of my hounds*: The Elizabethans took care in matching the voices of their hounds to sound in harmony together.

106 *Uncouple*: unleash; hounds, fastened together in pairs, were trained to keep silent when leashed.

107 *Dispatch*: see that it is done quickly.

108 *will*: will go.

109–10 *mark . . . conjunction*: listen to the mingled cry of hounds and echo together.

111–13 *I was . . . Sparta*: Hippolyta boasts of a superior hunting expedition with mythical companions: Crete and Sparta were both famous for the hounds they bred, but Cadmus (the founder of Thebes) belonged to a much earlier time than Hercules.

112 *bay'd the bear*: drove the bear to a position where it was forced to turn and face the hounds.

114 *chiding*: yelping.

118 *kind*: breed.

119 *flew'd*: with deep, hanging lips and cheeks.
sanded: with sand-colour markings.

121 *dewlapp'd*: with folds of skin (dew-laps) under their chins.
Thessalian: from Thessaly, a northern part of ancient Greece.

123 *cry*: pack of hounds.

124 *halloo*: the cry made by huntsmen in response to the hounds.
cheer'd: encouraged.

126 *soft*: wait a minute.
nymphs: creatures of the wood.

130 *of*: at.

131 *observe*: perform.

132 *our intent*: what we intended to do.

133 *in . . . solemnity*: to honour our celebration.

Wind horns. Enter Theseus *with* Hippolyta, Egeus, *and all his train*

Theseus
Go, one of you, find out the forester;
For now our observation is perform'd,
And since we have the vaward of the day,
105 My love shall hear the music of my hounds.
Uncouple in the western valley; let them go:
Dispatch, I say, and find the forester.
              [*Exit an* Attendant
We will, fair queen, up to the mountain's top,
And mark the musical confusion
110 Of hounds and echo in conjunction.
    Hippolyta
I was with Hercules and Cadmus once,
When in a wood of Crete they bay'd the bear
With hounds of Sparta: never did I hear
Such gallant chiding; for besides the groves,
115 The skies, the fountains, every region near
Seem'd all one mutual cry. I never heard
So musical a discord, such sweet thunder.
    Theseus
My hounds are bred out of the Spartan kind,
So flew'd, so sanded; and their heads are hung
120 With ears that sweep away the morning dew;
Crook-kneed, and dewlapp'd like Thessalian bulls;
Slow in pursuit, but match'd in mouth like bells,
Each under each. A cry more tuneable
Was never halloo'd to nor cheer'd with horn
125 In Crete, in Sparta, nor in Thessaly.
Judge when you hear. But soft, what nymphs are these?
    Egeus
My lord, this is my daughter here asleep,
And this Lysander; this Demetrius is,
This Helena, old Nedar's Helena.
130 I wonder of their being here together.
    Theseus
No doubt they rose up early to observe
The rite of May, and hearing our intent
Came here in grace of our solemnity.

But speak, Egeus; is not this the day
135 That Hermia should give answer of her choice?

Egeus
It is, my lord.

Theseus
Go, bid the huntsmen wake them with their horns.

Shout within; wind horns; the lovers all start up

137s.d. *all start up*: all jump to their feet.

Good morrow, friends. Saint Valentine is past;
Begin these woodbirds but to couple now?

138–9 *Saint Valentine . . . now*: It was
proverbially said that the birds chose
their partners on Saint Valentine's Day
(14 February).
139 *to couple*: to form pairs.

The lovers kneel

Lysander
140 Pardon, my lord.

Theseus
                    I pray you all, stand up.
I know you two are rival enemies:
How comes this gentle concord in the world,
That hatred is so far from jealousy

143 *jealousy*: suspicion.
144 *by hate*: by the side of one who hates
you.
145 *amazedly*: in confusion.

To sleep by hate, and fear no enmity?

Lysander
145 My lord, I shall reply amazedly,
Half sleep, half waking; but as yet, I swear,
I cannot truly say how I came here.
But as I think (for truly would I speak)
And now I do bethink me, so it is—
150 I came with Hermia hither. Our intent
Was to be gone from Athens, where we might

152 *Without*: out of reach of.

Without the peril of the Athenian law—

Egeus
Enough, enough, my lord; you have enough— ·
I beg the law, the law upon his head!

156 *defeated*: deprived.

155 They would have stol'n away, they would, Demetrius,
Thereby to have defeated you and me,
You of your wife, and me of my consent,
Of my consent that she should be your wife.

Demetrius

159 *stealth*: secret escape.
160 *purpose hither*: intention to come
here.

My lord, fair Helen told me of their stealth,
160 Of this their purpose hither to this wood;

162 *in fancy*: in her love.
163 *wot*: know.

166 *idle gaud*: worthless plaything.

168 *virtue*: power.

171 *ere*: before.
172 *like a sickness*: as though I were sick.
173 *come*: returned.

177 *anon*: presently.
178 *overbear*: overrule.

181 *something worn*: almost gone.
182 *purpos'd*: intended.

184 *solemnity*: celebration.

187 *turned*: turnèd.

188 *parted eye*: double vision (where the
eyes do not focus together).

And I in fury hither follow'd them,
Fair Helena in fancy following me.
But, my good lord, I wot not by what power
(But by some power it is), my love to Hermia,
165 Melted as the snow, seems to me now
As the remembrance of an idle gaud
Which in my childhood I did dote upon;
And all the faith, the virtue of my heart,
The object and the pleasure of mine eye,
170 Is only Helena. To her, my lord,
Was I betroth'd ere I saw Hermia;
But like a sickness did I loathe this food.
But, as in health come to my natural taste,
Now I do wish it, love it, long for it,
175 And will for evermore be true to it.

Theseus
Fair lovers, you are fortunately met.
Of this discourse we more will hear anon.
Egeus, I will overbear your will;
For in the temple, by and by, with us
180 These couples shall eternally be knit.
And, for the morning now is something worn,
Our purpos'd hunting shall be set aside.
Away with us to Athens. Three and three,
We'll hold a feast in great solemnity.
185 Come, Hippolyta.
            [*Exit* Theseus *with* Hippolyta, Egeus, *and his train*

Demetrius
These things seem small and undistinguishable,
Like far-off mountains turned into clouds.

Hermia
Methinks I see these things with parted eye,
When everything seems double.

Helena
                                    So methinks;
190 And I have found Demetrius, like a jewel,
Mine own, and not mine own.

Demetrius
                                    Are you sure
That we are awake? It seems to me

That yet we sleep, we dream. Do not you think
The duke was here, and bid us follow him?

Hermia

195 Yea, and my father.

Helena

And Hippolyta.

Lysander

And he did bid us follow to the temple.

Demetrius

Why, then, we are awake. Let's follow him,
And by the way let us recount our dreams.

[Exeunt lovers

Bottom *wakes*

Bottom

When my cue comes, call me, and I will answer. My next
200 is 'Most fair Pyramus'. Heigh ho! Peter Quince? Flute
the bellows-mender? Snout the tinker? Starveling?
God's my life! Stolen hence and left me asleep! I have
had a most rare vision. I have had a dream, past the wit
of man to say what dream it was. Man is but an ass if he
205 go about to expound this dream. Methought I was—
there is no man can tell what. Methought I was—and
methought I had—but man is but a patched fool if he
will offer to say what methought I had. The eye of man
hath not heard, the ear of man hath not seen, man's
210 hand is not able to taste, his tongue to conceive, nor his
heart to report what my dream was! I will get Peter
Quince to write a ballad of this dream; it shall be called
'Bottom's Dream', because it hath no bottom; and I will
sing it in the latter end of a play, before the duke.
215 Peradventure, to make it the more gracious, I shall sing
it at her death.

[Exit

199 *cue*: Bottom thinks he is still at the rehearsal.
next: i.e. next cue.

200 *Heigh ho!*: Bottom yawns—with a last vestige of the ass's 'Hee-haw!'.
205 *go about*: try.
expound: explain.
207 *patched fool*: Professional jesters wore multi-coloured garments, giving the effect of patchwork.
208–11 *The eye . . . dream was*: Bottom has vague (but appropriate) recollections of a biblical text: 'Eye hath not seen, nor ear heard . . . the things which God hath prepared for them that love him' (1 Corinthians 2:9–10).
212 *ballad*: Ballads, sung to existing tunes, were the sixteenth-century equivalent of modern newspapers.
213 *hath no bottom*: a) is without foundation in reality; b) is unfathomably profound.
215 *peradventure*: perhaps.
gracious: pleasing.
216 *her*: i.e. Thisbe's.

Act 4 Scene 2
Bottom returns to Athens, and the workmen
prepare to go to the palace.

2 *Out of doubt*: without doubt, certainly.
transported: carried away (by spirits).

3 *marred*: spoiled.

4 *forward*: ahead.

6 *discharge*: play the part of.

7 *wit*: intelligence.
handicraft man: craftsman.

9 *person*: personal appearance,
presence.
paramour: unlawful lover.

11 *paragon*: model of excellence.

12 *thing of naught*: something wicked or
immoral.

15 *gone forward*: taken place.
we . . . men: we would all have made
our fortunes.

16 *bully*: good fellow.

16–17 *sixpence . . . life*: A nobleman like
Theseus might reward distinguished
service with a regular pension for life;
'sixpence a day' was above average
pay for a skilled craftsman at this
time.

17 *'scaped*: missed.

18 *And*: if.

SCENE 2

Athens, a room in Quince's *house: enter* Quince,
Flute, Snout, *and* Starveling

Quince
Have you sent to Bottom's house? Is he come home yet?
Starveling
He cannot be heard of. Out of doubt he is transported.
Flute
If he come not, then the play is marred. It goes not
forward. Doth it?
Quince
5 It is not possible. You have not a man in all Athens able
to discharge Pyramus but he.
Flute
No, he hath simply the best wit of any handicraft man
in Athens.
Quince
Yea, and the best person, too; and he is a very paramour
10 for a sweet voice.
Flute
You must say 'paragon'. A paramour is (God bless us!) a
thing of naught.

Enter Snug *the joiner*

Snug
Masters, the duke is coming from the temple, and there
is two or three lords and ladies more married. If our
15 sport had gone forward, we had all been made men.
Flute
O, sweet bully Bottom! Thus hath he lost sixpence a day
during his life: he could not have 'scaped sixpence a day.
And the duke had not given him sixpence a day for
playing Pyramus, I'll be hanged. He would have
20 deserved it. Sixpence a day in Pyramus, or nothing.

Enter Bottom

Bottom

Where are these lads? Where are these hearts?

Quince

Bottom! O most courageous day! O most happy hour!

Bottom

Masters, I am to discourse wonders—but ask me not what; for if I tell you, I am not true Athenian. I will tell

25 you everything, right as it fell out.

Quince

Let us hear, sweet Bottom.

Bottom

Not a word of me. All that I will tell you is—that the duke hath dined. Get your apparel together, good strings to your beards, new ribbons to your pumps:

30 meet presently at the palace, every man look o'er his part. For the short and the long is, our play is preferred. In any case, let Thisbe have clean linen; and let not him that plays the lion pare his nails, for they shall hang out for the lion's claws. And, most dear actors, eat no onions

35 nor garlic; for we are to utter sweet breath, and I do not doubt but to hear them say it is a sweet comedy. No more words. Away! Go, away! [*Exeunt*

21 *hearts*: good fellows.

22 *courageous*: Quince perhaps means 'auspicious' (= favourable).
happy: lucky.

23 *I am to discourse wonders*: I have marvellous things to tell you.

25 *right . . . out*: exactly as it happened.

27 *of me*: about me.

28 *the duke hath dined*: This fixes the time of the scene: dinner was usually eaten at, or before, noon.
apparel: costumes.

29 *good strings*: i.e. to fasten them on.
pumps: dancing-shoes.

30 *presently*: immediately.

31 *preferred*: recommended.

32 *In any case*: whatever happens.

33 *pare*: clip.

35 *sweet breath*: pleasing words (which must not be spoiled by bad breath).

ACT 5

SCENE 1

Act 5 Scene 1
After their wedding Theseus and Hippolyta, with the other four lovers, watch the performance of 'Pyramus and Thisbe' before going to bed. When the mortals have retired, the fairies return to bless the marriages.

SCENE 1

Athens, the palace of Theseus: enter Theseus, Hippolyta, Philostrate, Lords *and* Attendants

3 *fairy toys*: silly tales about fairies.

4 *seething*: boiling, over-active.

5 *shaping fantasies*: inventive imaginations.
apprehend: conceive.

6 *comprehends*: understands.

7 *lunatic*: The word was particularly applied to those whose madness was brought on by changes of the moon (from Latin *luna* = moon).

8 *compact*: composed.

11 *Helen's beauty*: According to classical authors, Helen of Troy was the most beautiful woman in the world.
a brow of Egypt: the face of a gypsy (believed to originate from Egypt).

14 *bodies forth*: creates.

17 *local habitation*: particular dwelling-place.

20 *comprehends*: includes in its conception.

23–6 *But . . . constancy*: but the repeated accounts of the night, and the way their minds were all similarly affected ('transfigur'd') is evidence that there is more to this than fanciful invention, and it adds up to a great consistency.

27 *howsoever*: anyway.
admirable: to be marvelled at.

Hippolyta
'Tis strange, my Theseus, that these lovers speak of.
   Theseus
More strange than true. I never may believe
These antique fables, nor these fairy toys.
Lovers and madmen have such seething brains,
5 Such shaping fantasies, that apprehend
More than cool reason ever comprehends.
The lunatic, the lover, and the poet
Are of imagination all compact:
One sees more devils than vast hell can hold;
10 That is the madman. The lover, all as frantic,
Sees Helen's beauty in a brow of Egypt.
The poet's eye, in a fine frenzy rolling,
Doth glance from heaven to earth, from earth to heaven;
And as imagination bodies forth
15 The forms of things unknown, the poet's pen
Turns them to shapes, and gives to airy nothing
A local habitation and a name.
Such tricks hath strong imagination
That if it would but apprehend some joy,
20 It comprehends some bringer of that joy;
Or in the night, imagining some fear,
How easy is a bush supposed a bear?
   Hippolyta
But all the story of the night told over,
And all their minds transfigur'd so together,
25 More witnesseth than fancy's images,
And grows to something of great constancy;
But howsoever, strange and admirable.

Enter the lovers: Lysander, Demetrius, Hermia, *and* Helena

Theseus
Here come the lovers, full of joy and mirth.
Joy, gentle friends, joy and fresh days of love
30 Accompany your hearts!
    Lysander
                More than to us
Wait in your royal walks, your board, your bed!
    Theseus
Come now: what masques, what dances shall we have
To wear away this long age of three hours
Between our after-supper and bedtime?
35 Where is our usual manager of mirth?
What revels are in hand? Is there no play
To ease the anguish of a torturing hour?
Call Philostrate.
    Philostrate
                Here, mighty Theseus.
    Theseus
Say, what abridgement have you for this evening?
40 What masque, what music? How shall we beguile
The lazy time if not with some delight?
    Philostrate
[*Giving him a paper*] There is a brief how many sports
  are ripe.
Make choice of which your highness will see first.
    Theseus
[*Reading*] 'The battle with the Centaurs, to be sung
45 By an Athenian eunuch to the harp'—
We'll none of that; that have I told my love
In glory of my kinsman, Hercules.
[*Reading*] 'The riot of the tipsy Bacchanals,
Tearing the Thracian singer in their rage'—
50 That is an old device, and it was play'd
When I from Thebes came last a conqueror.
[*Reading*] 'The thrice three Muses mourning for the
  death
Of learning, late deceas'd in beggary'—
That is some satire keen and critical,

31 *walks*: wherever you go.
    board: table.
32 *masques*: entertainments with music and dancing.
33 *wear*: pass.
34 *after-supper*: Supper was a substantial meal, eaten usually about 5.30 p.m.
35 *manager of mirth*: Queen Elizabeth's Master of the Revels chose the plays for court performance, and saw them in rehearsal.
36 *revels*: amusements.
    in hand: available.
39 *abridgement*: pastime.
40 *beguile*: spend.
42 *brief*: programme.
    sports: entertainments.
    ripe: ready.
44 *battle with the Centaurs*: A story told in Ovid's *Metamorphoses*.
47 *kinsman*: Plutarch's 'Life of Theseus' says that he and Hercules, the Greek superman, were cousins 'by the mother side'.
48–9 *The riot . . . rage*: Orpheus, the Thracian poet, was torn to pieces by a drunken ('tipsy') mob of female followers of Bacchus, god of wine; the story is told in Ovid's *Metamorphoses*.
50 *device*: entertainment.
51 *from Thebes . . . conqueror*: In Chaucer's *Knight's Tale*, Theseus returns in triumph from Thebes with his prisoners.
52–3 *The thrice three . . . beggary*: This piece is now lost (if it ever existed); in classical mythology the Nine Muses are the patron goddesses of the different forms of art—and it is just possible that Shakespeare is making some allusion here to the recent ('late') death of Robert Greene, a writer and dramatist who died in poverty ('beggary') in 1592.
54 *keen*: biting.

55 *sorting with*: appropriate to.

60 *concord*: harmony.

65 *fitted*: suited to his role.

72 *Hard-handed men*: labourers (not
    gentlemen).
73 *labour'd in their minds*: engaged in
    intellectual exercise.
74 *unbreath'd*: untrained.
75 *against*: in preparation for.

77 *for you*: suitable for you.
    over: through.

79 *sport*: amusement.
    intent: intentions.
80 *stretch'd*: put to great effort.
    conn'd: learned by heart.
81 *do you service*: be of service to you.

82 *amiss*: wrong.

83 *simpleness*: artless sincerity.
    tender: offer.

55 Not sorting with a nuptial ceremony.
    [*Reading*] 'A tedious brief scene of young Pyramus
    And his love Thisbe, very tragical mirth'—
    Merry and tragical? Tedious and brief?
    That is hot ice and wondrous strange snow!
60 How shall we find the concord of this discord?
            Philostrate
    A play there is, my lord, some ten words long,
    Which is as 'brief' as I have known a play,
    But by ten words, my lord, it is too long,
    Which makes it 'tedious'. For in all the play
65 There is not one word apt, one player fitted.
    And 'tragical', my noble lord, it is,
    For Pyramus therein doth kill himself,
    Which when I saw rehears'd, I must confess,
    Made mine eyes water; but more 'merry' tears
70 The passion of loud laughter never shed.
            Theseus
    What are they that do play it?
            Philostrate
    Hard-handed men that work in Athens here,
    Which never labour'd in their minds till now;
    And now have toil'd their unbreath'd memories
75 With this same play against your nuptial.
            Theseus
    And we will hear it.
            Philostrate
                    No, my noble lord,
    It is not for you. I have heard it over,
    And it is nothing, nothing in the world,
    Unless you can find sport in their intents,
80 Extremely stretch'd, and conn'd with cruel pain,
    To do you service.
            Theseus
                    I will hear that play;
    For never anything can be amiss
    When simpleness and duty tender it.
    Go bring them in; and take your places, ladies.
                    [*Exit* Philostrate

85 *wretchedness*: inadequacy, disability.
   o'ercharg'd: overtaxed, overburdened.
86 *duty . . . perishing*: loyal servants
   failing in their efforts to please.

88 *they . . . kind*: they have no skill in
   this sort of thing.

90 *take*: take in good part, accept
   graciously.
91 *respect*: consideration.
92 *Takes . . . merit*: takes the will for the
   deed, judges the intention and not the
   accomplishment.
93 *Where . . . come*: in some places that
   I have visited.
   clerks: scholars.
   purposed: purposèd.
94 *premeditated welcomes*: carefully
   prepared speeches of welcome.
96 *periods*: full stops.
97 *Throttle*: choke.

101 *modesty*: embarrassment.
    fearful duty: frightened respect.
102 *rattling*: chattering.

104 *tongue-tied*: speechless.

105 *In least*: in few words.
    capacity: understanding.

106 *address'd*: ready to begin.

108–17 *If we offend . . . know*: Quince
    apparently reads from a scroll, making
    nonsense of the Prologue in exactly the
    way that Theseus described in line 96.
108 *will*: intention.
110 *But . . . skill*: Quince should read 'But
    with good will to show our simple
    skill'.

Hippolyta
85 I love not to see wretchedness o'ercharg'd,
   And duty in his service perishing.
   Theseus
   Why, gentle sweet, you shall see no such thing.
   Hippolyta
   He says they can do nothing in this kind.
   Theseus
   The kinder we, to give them thanks for nothing.
90 Our sport shall be to take what they mistake;
   And what poor duty cannot do, noble respect
   Takes it in might, not merit.
   Where I have come, great clerks have purposed
   To greet me with premeditated welcomes,
95 Where I have seen them shiver and look pale,
   Make periods in the midst of sentences,
   Throttle their practis'd accent in their fears,
   And in conclusion dumbly have broke off,
   Not paying me a welcome. Trust me, sweet,
100 Out of this silence yet I pick'd a welcome,
   And in the modesty of fearful duty
   I read as much as from the rattling tongue
   Of saucy and audacious eloquence.
   Love, therefore, and tongue-tied simplicity
105 In least speak most, to my capacity.

   Enter Philostrate

   Philostrate
   So please your grace, the Prologue is address'd.
   Theseus
   Let him approach.

   Flourish of trumpets

   Enter Quince *as* Prologue

   Quince
   If we offend, it is with our good will.
     That you should think, we come not to offend,
110 But with good will. To show our simple skill,

112 *but in despite*: not in ill-will, not to annoy you.
113 *minding*: meaning.

116 *at hand*: ready.
show: performance.

118 *stand upon*: pay attention to.
points: punctuation.

119 *rid*: ridden.
rough: unbroken.
120 *stop*: a) check in managing a horse;
b) punctuation mark; c) air-hole in a recorder.
121 *true*: properly.

123 *government*: control.

That is the true beginning of our end.
Consider then, we come but in despite.
We do not come as minding to content you,
Our true intent is. All for your delight,
115 We are not here. That you should here repent you,
The actors are at hand; and by their show
You shall know all that you are like to know.

Theseus
This fellow doth not stand upon points.

Lysander
He hath rid his prologue like a rough colt; he knows not
120 the stop. A good moral, my lord; it is not enough to
speak, but to speak true.

Hippolyta
Indeed, he hath played on this prologue like a child on a
recorder—a sound, but not in government.

Theseus
His speech was like a tangled chain, nothing impaired,
125 but all disordered. Who is next?

Enter with a Trumpeter *before them* Bottom *as*
Pyramus, Flute *as* Thisbe, Snout *as* Wall, Starveling
as Moonshine *and* Snug *as* Lion

Quince
[*as* Prologue] Gentles, perchance you wonder at this
show,
But wonder on, till truth make all things plain.
This man is Pyramus, if you would know;
This beauteous lady Thisbe is, certain.
130 This man with lime and rough-cast doth present
Wall, that vile wall which did these lovers sunder;
And through Wall's chink, poor souls they are content
To whisper—at the which let no man wonder.
This man with lanthorn, dog, and bush of thorn,
135 Presenteth Moonshine; for, if you will know,
By moonshine did these lovers think no scorn
To meet at Ninus' tomb, there, there to woo.
This grisly beast, which Lion hight by name,
The trusty Thisbe, coming first by night,
140 Did scare away, or rather did affright;

126 *Gentles*: Ladies and Gentlemen (the usual form of address to an audience).
perchance: perhaps.

134 *lanthorn*: An old form of 'lantern'.
dog . . . thorn: The thorn-bush is traditional (see *3, 1, 58*), but the dog is Shakespeare's invention.

138 *hight*: is called.

141 *fall*: drop.

143 *Anon*: presently.
   tall: brave.

145–6 *with blade . . . breast*: The excessive alliteration mocks the style of earlier English tragedy.
145 *Whereat*: whereupon.
   blade: sword.
146 *broach'd*: pierced.
147 *tarrying*: waiting.
149 *twain*: both.
150 *At large*: at full length.

151 *be to speak*: is going to speak.

153 *interlude*: short play.
   befall: happen.
154 *present*: represent.

156 *crannied*: cracked.

159 *this stone*: Snout is determined that the identity of 'Wall' should not be mistaken.
161 *sinister*: left; the word here is stressed on the second syllable.

163 *lime and hair*: The materials from which bricks were made.

164 *wittiest*: cleverest.
   partition: a) dividing wall; b) division of a speech or composition.

And as she fled, her mantle she did fall,
  Which Lion vile with bloody mouth did stain.
Anon comes Pyramus, sweet youth and tall,
  And finds his trusty Thisbe's mantle slain;
145 Whereat with blade, with bloody, blameful blade,
  He bravely broach'd his boiling bloody breast;
And Thisbe, tarrying in mulberry shade,
  His dagger drew, and died. For all the rest,
Let Lion, Moonshine, Wall, and lovers twain
150 At large discourse, while here they do remain.
    [*Exeunt* Quince, Bottom, Flute, Snug, *and* Starveling
    Theseus
I wonder if the lion be to speak?
    Demetrius
No wonder, my lord; one lion may, when many asses do.
    Snout
[*as* Wall] In this same interlude it doth befall
That I, one Snout by name, present a wall;
155 And such a wall as I would have you think
That had in it a crannied hole or chink,
Through which the lovers, Pyramus and Thisbe,
Did whisper often, very secretly.
This loam, this rough-cast, and this stone doth show
160 That I am that same wall; the truth is so.
And this the cranny is, right and sinister,
Through which the fearful lovers are to whisper.
    Theseus
Would you desire lime and hair to speak better?
    Demetrius
It is the wittiest partition that ever I heard discourse, my
165 lord.

    Enter Bottom *as* Pyramus

    Theseus
Pyramus draws near the wall; silence!
    Bottom
[*as* Pyramus] O grim-look'd night, O night with hue
  so black,
  O night which ever art when day is not!
O night, O night, alack, alack, alack,

'I see a voice; now will I to the chink' (5, 1, 188). Daniel Evans as Flute/Thisbe, Howard Crossley as Snout/Wall, and Desmond Barrit as Bottom/Pyramus, Royal Shakespeare Company, 1995.

170   I fear my Thisbe's promise is forgot!
    And thou, O wall, O sweet, O lovely wall,
       That stand'st between her father's ground and mine,
    Thou wall, O wall, O sweet and lovely wall,
       Show me thy chink, to blink through with mine eyne.
      [Wall *parts his fingers*]

174 *eyne*: eyes.

175 Thanks, courteous wall; Jove shield thee well for this!
    But what see I? No Thisbe do I see.
    O wicked wall, through whom I see no bliss,
      Curs'd be thy stones for thus deceiving me!
      Theseus
The wall, methinks, being sensible, should curse again.
      Bottom

179 *sensible*: capable of feeling.
    again: in reply.

180 No, in truth sir, he should not. 'Deceiving me' is Thisbe's
cue. She is to enter now, and I am to spy her through the
wall. You shall see it will fall pat as I told you. Yonder she
comes.

182 *fall*: happen.
    pat: exactly.

Enter Flute *as* Thisbe

      Flute
[*as* Thisbe] O wall, full often hast thou heard my
    moans,
185   For parting my fair Pyramus and me.
My cherry lips have often kiss'd thy stones,
    Thy stones with lime and hair knit up in thee.
      Bottom
[*as* Pyramus] I see a voice; now will I to the chink,
    To spy and I can hear my Thisbe's face.
190 Thisbe!
      Flute
[*as* Thisbe] My love! Thou art my love, I think?
      Bottom
[*as* Pyramus] Think what thou wilt, I am thy lover's
    grace,
And like Limander am I trusty still.
      Flute
[*as* Thisbe] And I like Helen, till the Fates me kill.
      Bottom
[*as* Pyramus] Not Shafalus to Procrus was so true.

189 *and*: if.
192 *lover's grace*: gracious lover.
193 *Limander*: Leander, the lover in Greek
mythology who drowned whilst
swimming the Hellespont to reach his
beloved, Hero—whom Flute confuses
with 'Helen'.
194 *Helen*: i.e. Helen of Troy, who was
stolen away from her husband by the
Trojan warrior, Paris.
    Fates: Three sister goddesses in Greek
mythology who were said to spin,
draw, and cut the thread of human
life.

195 *Shafalus . . . Procrus*: A story in Ovid's *Metamorphoses* tells how Cephalus by mistake killed his faithful wife Procris with a javelin that she had given him.

198 *Ninny's tomb*: Pyramus (Bottom) repeats Flute's blunder (*3*, 1, 83). *straightway*: immediately.

199 *Tide*: betide, come.

200 *discharged*: dischargèd; performed.

202 *mural*: wall.

203 *No remedy*: there is no help for it.

206 *The best . . . shadows*: even the best actors are no more than shadows—the creations and creators of dreams, visions, and illusions (compare Puck's epilogue, 406–11).
207 *amend them*: make up for their deficiencies.

210 *pass for*: be counted as.
211 *in*: on to the stage.

Flute
195 [*as* Thisbe] As Shafalus to Procrus, I to you.
Bottom
[*as* Pyramus] O, kiss me through the hole of this vile wall!
Flute
[*as* Thisbe] I kiss the wall's hole, not your lips at all.
Bottom
[*as* Pyramus] Wilt thou at Ninny's tomb meet me straightway?
Flute
[*as* Thisbe] Tide life, tide death, I come without delay.
[*Exeunt* Bottom *and* Flute *in different directions*
Snout
200 [*as* Wall] Thus have I, Wall, my part discharged so;
And being done, thus Wall away doth go.   [*Exit*
Theseus
Now is the mural down between the two neighbours.
Demetrius
No remedy, my lord, when walls are so wilful to hear without warning.
Hippolyta
205 This is the silliest stuff that ever I heard.
Theseus
The best in this kind are but shadows; and the worst are no worse, if imagination amend them.
Hippolyta
It must be your imagination then, and not theirs.
Theseus
If we imagine no worse of them than they of
210 themselves, they may pass for excellent men. Here come two noble beasts in, a man and a lion.

Enter Snug *as* Lion *and* Starveling *as* Moonshine

Snug
[*as* Lion] You ladies, you whose gentle hearts do fear
   The smallest monstrous mouse that creeps on floor,
May now, perchance, both quake and tremble here,
215   When Lion rough in wildest rage doth roar.
Then know that I as Snug the joiner am

217 *fell*: savage.
   dam: mother.

219 *'twere . . . life*: I would be in danger of
   losing my life.

220 *gentle*: polite.

222 *very*: real, true.
222-3 *lion . . . fox . . . goose*: These
   creatures were proverbial for their
   valour, cunning ('discretion'), and
   stupidity.

224-5 *carry his discretion*: support his
   judgement.
225 *carries*: carries off.

229 *horned*: hornèd; crescent moon.
230 *He . . . head*: i.e. like a cuckold: it
   was a commonplace joke that men
   with unfaithful wives would grow
   horns on their heads.
231-2 *within the circumference*: inside
   the full circle.

233 *horned*: hornèd.
235-6 *the man . . . lantern*: It is known
   that the actor who first played
   Starveling was very thin.

238 *for*: for fear of.
239 *in snuff*: a) in need of snuffing out;
   b) angry.

A lion fell, nor else no lion's dam;
For if I should as lion come in strife
Into this place, 'twere pity on my life.
   Theseus
220 A very gentle beast, and of a good conscience.
   Demetrius
The very best at a beast, my lord, that e'er I saw.
   Lysander
This lion is a very fox for his valour.
   Theseus
True; and a goose for his discretion.
   Demetrius
Not so, my lord; for his valour cannot carry his
225 discretion; and the fox carries the goose.
   Theseus
His discretion, I am sure, cannot carry his valour; for
the goose carries not the fox. It is well: leave it to his
discretion, and let us listen to the moon.
   Starveling
[*as* Moonshine] This lanthorn doth the horned moon
   present—
   Demetrius
230 He should have worn the horns on his head.
   Theseus
He is no crescent, and his horns are invisible within the
circumference.
   Starveling
[*as* Moonshine] This lanthorn doth the horned moon
   present;
   Myself the man i'th'moon do seem to be—
   Theseus
235 This is the greatest error of all the rest; the man should
be put into the lantern. How is it else the man
i'th'moon?
   Demetrius
He dares not come there, for the candle; for you see it is
already in snuff.
   Hippolyta
240 I am aweary of this moon. Would he would change!

242 *in courtesy*: it is polite.
   in all reason: it is only reasonable.
242–3 *stay the time*: wait until the play is
   over.

245–7 *All . . . dog*: The comments from
   his audience have driven Starveling
   into prose.

Theseus
It appears by his small light of discretion that he is in
the wane; but yet in courtesy, in all reason, we must stay
the time.
   Lysander
Proceed, Moon.
   Starveling
245 All that I have to say is to tell you that the lanthorn is the
moon, I the man i'th'moon, this thorn bush my thorn
bush, and this dog my dog.
   Demetrius
Why, all these should be in the lantern, for all these are
in the moon. But silence: here comes Thisbe.

   Enter Flute *as* Thisbe

   Flute
250 [*as* Thisbe] This is old Ninny's tomb. Where is my
      love?
   Snug
[*as* Lion] O!
         Lion *roars.* [Thisbe *runs off dropping her mantle*
   Demetrius
Well roared, Lion!
   Theseus
Well run, Thisbe!
   Hippolyta
Well shone, Moon! Truly, the moon shines with a good
255 grace.
   Theseus
Well moused, Lion!
   Demetrius
And then came Pyramus—
   Lysander
And so the lion vanished.
         [Lion *worries* Thisbe*'s mantle, and exit*

256 *Well moused*: Lion must have been
   pawing the garment as a cat shakes a
   mouse.

Enter Bottom *as* Pyramus

Bottom
[*as* Pyramus] Sweet moon, I thank thee for thy sunny
    beams;
260   I thank thee, moon, for shining now so bright;
For by thy gracious, golden, glittering gleams
    I trust to take of truest Thisbe sight.
      But stay—O spite!
      But mark, poor knight,
265   What dreadful dole is here?
      Eyes, do you see?
      How can it be?
    O dainty duck, O dear!
      Thy mantle good—
270   What, stain'd with blood?
    Approach, ye Furies fell!
      O Fates, come, come,
      Cut thread and thrum,
    Quail, crush, conclude, and quell.
Theseus
275 This passion, and the death of a dear friend, would go
near to make a man look sad.
Hippolyta
Beshrew my heart, but I pity the man.
Bottom
[*as* Pyramus] O wherefore, Nature, didst thou lions
    frame,
    Since lion vile hath here deflower'd my dear?
280 Which is—no, no—which was the fairest dame
    That liv'd, that lov'd, that lik'd, that look'd with cheer.
      Come tears, confound!
      Out sword, and wound
    The pap of Pyramus,
285   Ay, that left pap,
      Where heart doth hop:
    Thus die I, thus, thus, thus! [*Stabs himself*]
      Now am I dead,
      Now am I fled;
290   My soul is in the sky.
      Tongue, lose thy light;

263 *spite*: disaster.

265 *dole*: cause for grief.

271 *Furies fell*: The avenging goddesses of Greek mythology who were remorseless ('fell') in their pursuit of evildoers.
272 *Fates*: See line 194note.
273 *thread and thrum*: i.e. good and bad; the 'thrum' is the waste left on the weaver's loom when the woven fabric is removed.
274 *Quail*: overpower.
    quell: slay.
277 *Beshrew*: curse.

278 *frame*: construct.
279 *deflower'd*: ravished, carried off.

281 *look'd with cheer*: looked with her face.
282 *confound*: destroy.

284 *pap*: breast.

Moon, take thy flight;   [*Exit* Starveling

Now die, die, die, die, die. [*He dies*]

Demetrius

No die, but an ace for him; for he is but one.

Lysander

295   Less than an ace, man; for he is dead, he is nothing.

Theseus

With the help of a surgeon he might yet recover, and yet

prove an ass.

Hippolyta

How chance Moonshine is gone before Thisbe comes

back and finds her lover?

Theseus

300   She will find him by starlight.

Enter Flute *as* Thisbe

Here she comes and her passion ends the play.

Hippolyta

Methinks she should not use a long one for such a

Pyramus; I hope she will be brief.

Demetrius

A mote will turn the balance, which Pyramus, which

305   Thisbe is the better: he for a man, God warrant us; she

for a woman, God bless us.

Lysander

She hath spied him already, with those sweet eyes.

Demetrius

And thus she means, videlicet—

Flute

[*as* Thisbe] Asleep, my love?

310   What, dead, my dove?

O Pyramus, arise.

        Speak, speak! Quite dumb?

        Dead, dead? A tomb

Must cover thy sweet eyes.

315   These lily lips,

        This cherry nose,

These yellow cowslip cheeks

        Are gone, are gone.

        Lovers, make moan;

320   His eyes were green as leeks.

294 *die*: one of a pair of dice.
  ace: the single spot on a dice.

298 *How chance*: how does it happen that.

304 *mote*: speck of dust.
304–5 *which . . . Thisbe*: whether Pyramus
  or Thisbe.
305 *warrant*: defend.

307 *spied*: caught sight of.

308 *means*: moans.
  videlicet: namely.

321 *sisters three*: See line 194note.

324 *gore*: blood.

329 *imbrue*: pierce.

333 *left*: left alive.

337 *Bergomask dance*: A country dance originating in Bergamo, in northern Italy.

339 *No . . . excuse*: It was customary in the epilogue to ask the audience to pardon the play's shortcomings—as Puck does at the end of *A Midsummer Night's Dream*.
341 *Marry*: by the Virgin Mary.
writ: wrote.
344 *notably*: commendably.
discharged: performed.
344–5 *let . . . alone*: forget about the epilogue.

346 *iron tongue*: i.e. of a bell.
told: tolled, chimed; counted.
348 *outsleep*: sleep late.
349 *overwatch'd*: stayed up late.
350 *palpable-gross*: dreadfully crude.
350–1 *beguil'd . . . night*: amused us so that we did not feel that time was passing slowly tonight.
352 *solemnity*: celebration.
353 *In nightly revels*: with entertainments every night.

O sisters three,
Come, come to me
With hands as pale as milk;
Lay them in gore,
325 Since you have shore
With shears his thread of silk.
Tongue, not a word!
Come, trusty sword,
Come blade, my breast imbrue! [*Stabs herself*]
330 And farewell, friends.
Thus Thisbe ends—
Adieu, adieu, adieu! [*Dies*]
Theseus
Moonshine and Lion are left to bury the dead.
Demetrius
Ay, and Wall, too.
Bottom
335 [*Starting up, as* Flute *does also*] No, I assure you, the wall is down that parted their fathers. Will it please you to see the epilogue, or to hear a Bergomask dance between two of our company?
Theseus
No epilogue, I pray you; for your play needs no excuse.
340 Never excuse; for when the players are all dead, there need none to be blamed. Marry, if he that writ it had played Pyramus and hanged himself in Thisbe's garter, it would have been a fine tragedy: and so it is, truly, and very notably discharged. But come, your Bergomask; let
345 your epilogue alone.

The company return; two of them dance, then exeunt
Bottom, Flute, and their fellows

The iron tongue of midnight hath told twelve.
Lovers, to bed; 'tis almost fairy time.
I fear we shall outsleep the coming morn
As much as we this night have overwatch'd.
350 This palpable-gross play hath well beguil'd
The heavy gait of night. Sweet friends, to bed.
A fortnight hold we this solemnity
In nightly revels and new jollity.   [*Exeunt*

Enter Puck *carrying a broom*

Puck
Now the hungry lion roars,
And the wolf behowls the moon,
Whilst the heavy ploughman snores,
All with weary task foredone.
Now the wasted brands do glow,
Whilst the screech-owl, screeching loud,
Puts the wretch that lies in woe
In remembrance of a shroud.
Now it is the time of night
That the graves, all gaping wide,
Every one lets forth his sprite
In the church-way paths to glide.
And we fairies, that do run
By the triple Hecate's team
From the presence of the sun,
Following darkness like a dream,
Now are frolic; not a mouse
Shall disturb this hallow'd house.
I am sent with broom before
To sweep the dust behind the door.

Enter Oberon *and* Titania, *the King and Queen of
Fairies, with all their train*

Oberon
Through the house give glimmering light
By the dead and drowsy fire;
Every elf and fairy sprite
Hop as light as bird from briar,
And this ditty after me
Sing, and dance it trippingly.
Titania
First rehearse your song by rote,
To each word a warbling note;
Hand in hand with fairy grace
Will we sing and bless this place.

Song and dance

355
360
365
370
375
380

355 *behowls*: howls at.
356 *heavy*: exhausted.
357 *foredone*: tired out.
358 *wasted*: burnt out.
  brands: logs of wood (on the fire).
359–61 *the screech-owl . . . shroud*: The
  Elizabethans believed that the owl's
  cry was ominous, foretelling death.

364 *his sprite*: the ghost of the man buried
  there.

367 *triple Hecate*: The goddess of night
  and witchcraft, who had three
  identities: Luna in heaven, Diana on
  earth, and Hecate (pronounced here
  with only two syllables) in the
  underworld.
370 *frolic*: playful.
372 *with broom*: Robin Goodfellow
  (*2, 1, 34*) was traditionally
  represented with a broom.
  before: ahead of the fairies.

374 *glimmering*: flickering.

376 *sprite*: spirit.

377 *ditty*: song.

380 *rehearse . . . rote*: repeat your song
  from memory.

Oberon

Now until the break of day
385 Through this house each fairy stray.
To the best bride-bed will we,
Which by us shall blessed be;
And the issue there create
Ever shall be fortunate.
390 So shall all the couples three
Ever true in loving be,
And the blots of nature's hand
Shall not in their issue stand.
Never mole, harelip, nor scar,
395 Nor mark prodigious, such as are
Despised in nativity,
Shall upon their children be.
With this field-dew consecrate,
Every fairy take his gait,
400 And each several chamber bless
Through this palace with sweet peace;
And the owner of it bless'd
Ever shall in safety rest.
Trip away, make no stay;
405 Meet me all by break of day.

[*Exeunt all but* Puck

Puck

[*To the audience*] If we shadows have offended,
Think but this, and all is mended:
That you have but slumber'd here
While these visions did appear;
410 And this weak and idle theme,
No more yielding but a dream,
Gentles, do not reprehend;
If you pardon, we will mend.
And, as I am an honest Puck,
415 If we have unearned luck
Now to 'scape the serpent's tongue
We will make amends ere long,
Else the Puck a liar call.
So, good night unto you all.
420 Give me your hands, if we be friends,
And Robin shall restore amends.

[*Exit*

386 *best bride-bed*: i.e. that of Theseus and Hippolyta.
387 *blessed*: blessèd.
388 *issue*: children.
    create: conceive.
389 *fortunate*: lucky.

392 *blots*: mistakes.

393 *stand*: be seen.

395 *mark prodigious*: ominous birthmark (thought to foretell bad luck for the child).
    Despised: despisèd.
398 *consecrate*: consecrated.
399 *take his gait*: make his way.
400 *several*: separate.

406 *shadows*: a) fairies; b) actors. Compare line 206.

410 *idle*: foolish.
411 *no more yielding*: producing no more profit.
412 *Gentles*: ladies and gentlemen—a courteous address to the audience.
    reprehend: reproach.
413 *mend*: improve.
415 *unearned*: unearnèd; undeserved.
416 *'scape*: escape.
    the serpent's tongue: the hissing that indicates an audience's disapproval.
417 *make amends*: repay you.
    ere: before.
418 *the Puck*: See 'Leading Characters in the Play', p.vii.
420 *give me your hands*: i.e applaud.
421 *restore amends*: give satisfaction in return.

'Give me your hands, if we be friends, And Robin shall restore amends.' (*5*, 1, 420–1) Aidan McArdle as Puck, Royal Shakespeare Company, 1999.

Background

England in 1595

When Shakespeare was writing *A Midsummer Night's Dream*, many people still believed that the sun went round the earth. They were taught that this was the way God had ordered things, and that – in England – God had founded a Church and appointed a Monarchy so that the land and people could be well governed.

'The past is a foreign country; they do things differently there.'

L. P. Hartley

Government

For most of Shakespeare's life, the reigning monarch of England was Queen Elizabeth I. With her counsellors and ministers, she governed the nation from London, although fewer than half a million people out of a total population of six million lived in the capital city. In the rest of the country, law and order were maintained by the land-owners and enforced by their deputies. The average man had no vote, and women had no rights at all.

Religion

At this time, England was a Christian country. All children were baptized, soon after they were born, into the Church of England; they were taught the essentials of the Christian faith, and instructed in their duty to God and to humankind. Marriages and funerals were conducted only by the licensed clergy and according to the Church's rites and ceremonies. Attending divine service was compulsory; absences (without a good medical reason) could be punished by fines. By such means, the authorities were able to keep some control over the population – recording births, marriages, and deaths; being alert to anyone who refused to accept standard religious practices, who could be politically dangerous; and ensuring that people received the approved teachings through the official 'Homilies' which were regularly preached in all parish churches.

Elizabeth I's father, Henry VIII, had broken away from the Church of Rome, and from that time all people in England were able to hear the church services *in their own language* rather than in Latin. The Book of Common Prayer was used in every church, and an English translation of the Bible was read aloud in public. The Christian religion had never been so well taught before!

Education

School education reinforced the Church's teaching. From the age of four, boys might attend the 'petty school' (its name came from the French '*petite école*') to learn reading and writing along with a few prayers; some schools also included work with numbers. At the age of seven, the boy was ready for the grammar school (if his father was willing and able to pay the fees).

Grammar schools taught Latin grammar, translation work and the study of Roman authors, paying attention as much to style as to content. The art of fine writing was therefore important from early youth. A very few students went on to university; these were either clever boys who won scholarships, or else the sons of rich noblemen. Girls stayed at home, and learned domestic and social skills – cooking, sewing, perhaps even music. The lucky ones might learn to read and write.

Language

At the start of the sixteenth century the English had a very poor opinion of their own language: there was little serious writing in English, and hardly any literature. Latin was the language of international scholarship, and the eloquent style of the Romans was much admired. Many translations from Latin were made, and in this way writers increased the vocabulary of English and made its grammar more flexible. French, Italian, and Spanish works were also translated and, for the first time, there were English versions of the Bible. By the end of the century, English was a language to be proud of: it was rich in vocabulary, capable of infinite variety and subtlety, and ready for all kinds of word-play – especially *puns*, for which Elizabethan English is renowned.

Drama

The great art-form of the Elizabethan and Jacobean age was its drama. The Elizabethans inherited a tradition of play-acting from the Middle Ages, and they reinforced this by reading and translating the Roman playwrights. At the beginning of the sixteenth century plays were performed by groups of actors. These were all-male companies (boys acted the female roles) who travelled from town to town, setting up their stages in open places (such as inn-yards) or, with the permission of the owner, in the hall of some noble house. The touring companies continued outside London into the seventeenth century; but in London, in 1576, a new building was erected for the performance of plays. This was the Theatre, the first purpose-built playhouse in England. Other playhouses followed, including the Globe, where most of Shakespeare's plays were performed, and English drama reached new heights.

There were people who disapproved, of course. The theatres, which brought large crowds together, could encourage the spread of disease – and dangerous ideas. During the summer, when the plague was at its worst, the playhouses were closed. A constant censorship was imposed, more or less severe at different times. The Puritans, a religious and political faction who wanted to impose strict rules of behaviour, tried to close down the theatres. However, partly because the royal family favoured drama, and partly because the buildings were outside the city limits, they did not succeed until 1642.

Theatre

From contemporary comments and sketches – most particularly a drawing by a Dutch visitor, Johannes de Witt – it is possible to form some idea of the typical Elizabethan playhouse for which most of Shakespeare's plays were written. Hexagonal (six-sided) in shape, it had three roofed galleries encircling an open courtyard. The plain, high stage projected into the yard, where it was surrounded by the audience of standing 'groundlings'. At the back were two doors for the actors' entrances and exits; and above these doors was a balcony – useful for a musicians' gallery or for the acting of scenes *above*. Over the stage was a

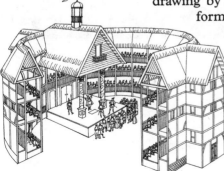

thatched roof, supported on two pillars, forming a canopy – which seems to have been painted with the sun, moon, and stars for the 'heavens'.

Underneath was space (concealed by curtains) which could be used by characters ascending and descending through a trap-door in the stage. Costumes and properties were kept backstage in the 'tiring house'. The actors used the most luxurious costumes they could find, often clothes given to them by rich patrons. Stage properties were important for showing where a scene was set, but the dramatist's own words were needed to explain the time of day, since all performances took place in the early afternoon.

A replica of Shakespeare's own theatre, the Globe, has been built in London, and stands in Southwark, almost exactly on the Bankside site of the original.

William Shakespeare, 1564–1616

Elizabeth I was Queen of England when Shakespeare was born in 1564. He was the son of a tradesman who made and sold gloves in the small town of Stratford-upon-Avon, and he was educated at the grammar school in that town. Shakespeare did not go to university when he left school, but worked, perhaps, in his father's business. When he was eighteen he married Anne Hathaway, who became the mother of his daughter, Susanna, in 1583, and of twins in 1585.

There is nothing exciting, or even unusual, in this story; and from 1585 until 1592 there are no documents that can tell us anything at all about Shakespeare. But we have learned that in 1592 he was known in London, and that he had become both an actor and a playwright.

We do not know when Shakespeare wrote his first play, and we are not sure of the order in which he wrote his works. If you look on page 91 at the list of his writings and their approximate dates, you will see he started by writing plays on subjects taken from the history of England. No doubt this was partly because he was patriotic and interested in English history, but he was also a very shrewd businessman. He could see that the theatre audiences enjoyed being shown their own history, and it was certain that he would make a profit from this kind of drama.

He also wrote comedies, with romantic love-stories of young people who fall in love with one another, and at the end of the play marry and live happily ever after.

At the end of the sixteenth century Shakespeare wrote some melancholy, bitter, and tragic plays. This change may have been caused by some sadness in the writer's life (his only son died in 1596). Shakespeare, however, was not the only writer whose works at this time were very serious. The whole of England was facing a crisis. Queen Elizabeth I was growing old. She was greatly loved, and the people were sad to think she must soon die; they were also afraid, because the queen had never married, and so there was no child to succeed her.

When James I, Elizabeth's Scottish cousin, came to the throne in 1603, Shakespeare continued to write serious drama — the great tragedies and the plays based on Roman history (such as *Julius Caesar*) for which he is most famous. Finally, before he retired from the theatre, he wrote another set of comedies. These all have the same theme: they tell of happiness which is lost, and then found again.

Shakespeare returned from London to Stratford, his home town. He was rich and successful, and he owned one of the biggest houses in the town. He died in 1616.

Shakespeare also wrote two long poems, and a collection of sonnets. The sonnets describe two love affairs, but we do not know who the lovers were – or whether they existed only in Shakespeare's imagination. Although there are many public documents concerned with his career as a writer and a businessman, Shakespeare has hidden his personal life from us. A nineteenth-century poet, Matthew Arnold, addressed Shakespeare in a poem, and wrote 'We ask and ask – Thou smilest, and art still'.

There is not even a portrait of the world's greatest dramatist that we can be sure is really of Shakespeare, and painted by someone who had seen him.

Approximate Dates of Composition of Shakespeare's Works

Period	Comedies	History plays	Tragedies	Poems
I before 1594	Comedy of Errors Taming of the Shrew Two Gentlemen of Verona Love's Labour's Lost	Henry VI, part 1 Henry VI, part 2 Henry VI, part 3 Richard III	Titus Andronicus	Venus and Adonis Rape of Lucrece
II 1594 – 1599	Midsummer Night's Dream Merchant of Venice Merry Wives of Windsor Much Ado About Nothing As You Like It	Richard II King John Henry IV, part 1 Henry IV, part 2 Henry V	Romeo and Juliet	Sonnets
III 1599 – 1608	Twelfth Night Troilus and Cressida Measure for Measure All's Well That Ends Well Pericles		Julius Caesar Hamlet Othello Timon of Athens King Lear Macbeth Antony and Cleopatra Coriolanus	
IV 1608 – 1613	Cymbeline The Winter's Tale The Tempest	Henry VIII		

Exploring A Midsummer Night's Dream in the Classroom

With entangled sub-plots weaving stories of romance and resentment, together with muddles and mischief, *A Midsummer Night's Dream* is a delight to study in the classroom.

This section suggests a range of approaches in the classroom, to help bring the text to life and engender both enjoyment and understanding of the play.

Ways into the Play

Students may feel an antipathy towards the study of Shakespeare. The imaginative and enthusiastic teacher, with the help of this edition of the play, will soon break this down!

Three wishes

Awaken a magical mood amongst your students by acting as a fairy godmother or genie, and giving them three wishes. Give them time to discuss and share their ideas. Whether you can grant their wishes or not is a different matter!

Pictures

Every picture tells a story, so ask your students to look at the picture on the front cover of this book and guess who the people are and what is happening. Once they are more familiar with the play, ask them to hazard a guess as to the exact moment in the play that is depicted.

Navigating the play

Your students may need some help and practice at finding their way around a Shakespeare play. After explaining the division into acts, scenes and lines, challenge them to look up some references as quickly as possible. Refer them to some of the famous lines and those that might lead on to further discussion of the plot. Below are some suggestions.

Act 1, Scene i, line 134   *The course of true love never did run smooth*

Act II, Scene i, line 60   *Ill met by moonlight, proud Titania!*
Act III, Scene ii, line 282–3 *O me, you juggler, you canker-blossom,*
                        You thief of love!

Improvisation Working on one of these improvisations may help students to access some of the ideas behind the drama.

a)   Students can improvise a conversation between a parent and teenager. The parent has arranged something for the son/daughter (e.g. a holiday, a day out, a party), but the teenager refuses to go. Both are convinced that they are in the right and refuse to back down. Discuss how it feels to be each person.

b)   Two friends A and B are in conversation (the students can think up the topic). Friend A engages with the other in a chatty way. However, Friend B blows hot and cold. He or she starts off being interested and friendly, but changes (at will or at a signal) to being cold, disinterested, or even rude. Discuss how this feels for A and the reasons that B might be so changeable.

c)   Friend A tells Friend B a secret (e.g. he or she's arranged to go to a party without telling his or her parents). Friend B doesn't keep the secret, but tells the other person(s) involved. Pairs should improvise the conversation that takes place when A finds out.

Setting the Scene

Designing the set There are two main settings for the play:

- a palace in Athens where life is courtly and well-ordered
- the forest – the realm of the fairies, the setting for love, magic, and a little madness.

Ask your students to research ideas and design two stage sets which show the contrasting worlds. A front view of the stage is probably easiest. The students can annotate their designs to explain their ideas.

Classical characters The play opens on the theme of marriage. Duke Theseus, who won Hippolyta by force, is arranging their wedding. These two characters are based on mythological figures (see page vii). Ask the students to research the origins of the two characters. Then discuss the tensions behind their relationship and the influence this may have on the play.

Fathers and daughters 'To you your father should be as a god', Theseus tells Hermia (*1*, 1, 47). Your students may need to be made aware of the submissive role that Elizabethan women were expected to take to either their father or their husband. Discuss how much things have changed. Do they treat their parents with this sort of respect? How does modern-day marriage hark back to the past (e.g. the father giving away the bride)?

Keeping Track of the Action

It's important to give your students opportunities to 'digest' and reflect upon their reading, so that they can take ownership of the play.

Reading journals As you read through the play, help students to trace and understand the main plot and sub-plots by asking them to keep a journal each, in which they record what happens. They might keep a page to trace each strand of the story: the lovers, the workmen, the fairy world. They can also record their reactions and thoughts about the action and the characters. Their responses can be kept focused through specific questions from the teacher.

A play within a play The workmen are planning and rehearsing 'The most lamentable comedy and the most cruel death of Pyramus and Thisbe' for the Duke's wedding. Encourage your students to follow the workmen's progress by creating the necessary publicity (e.g. programmes and posters) and resources (e.g. set design, costume, and prop designs).

Horoscopes Fortunes change very suddenly in this play and much of the action takes place under the moon and stars in a magical wood. Ask your students to write horoscopes for different characters at various points in the action. Some suggestions are:

Act I, Scene i	(Hermia's future is uncertain, her love life looks bleak and she doesn't know whom can she trust)
Act III, Scene i	(Bottom finds unexpected romance, but needs to look to his appearance)
Act III, Scene ii	(Helena finds popularity, but is everything as it seems?)

Ideally the horoscopes should have some ambiguity and humour, reflecting both the students' grasp of the plot and the characters' fates.

Different versions Prose versions, film adaptations and audio recordings are all excellent aids to tracking the plot. Leon Garfield's story (see 'Further Reading and Resources', page 100) uses exquisite prose. Marcia Williams' picture book (see 'Further Reading and Resources', page 100) is a delightful version for any age and is particularly useful for engaging less able students. Audio versions, such as the BBC audio CD/tape (see 'Further Reading and Resources', page 101) are excellent for listening to whilst the students follow the text.

Looking at such aspects as film techniques, music, and costumes can stimulate students to create their own interpretations.

DVD versions mean that effective still shots can be captured and analysed, giving even greater insight into the filmmakers' skills. For example, analysing a still from Hoffman's film (1998), such as the scene where Egeus brings Hermia before the Duke, will reveal both the dynamics and relationships within the scene, as well as the meticulous and painterly interpretation of the filmmaker.

GCSE students may be able to develop this into a piece of coursework that examines a director's interpretation of the play (or part of the play).

Characters

Students of all ages need to come to an understanding of the characters: their motivations, their relationships, and their development.

Magic and mayhem cards Students need to be aware of the powerful and often menacing nature of the creatures known as fairies. Despite some of the names, they are not the gentile, delicate creatures of children's stories. They hold potent magic and a controlling, invisible sway on human lives. As Puck shows, they can also be meddlesome and mischievous.

Ask your students to create profiles of the fairies. For younger students, these profiles could be in the form the popular gaming cards such as 'Top Trumps', where characters are illustrated and given ratings for such attributes as: strength, intelligence, magic, mischief, etc.

The workmen As is often the case with Shakespeare, the names of the characters are revealing. Ask your students to investigate the names of the workman, their literal meanings (see page viii) and the connotations/associations of the names.

A different perspective Allowing your students the opportunity to think, write, and talk as one of the characters gives them a new and illuminating perspective on the characters. Here are some possible scenarios.

a)   Hermia leaves a note to her father, explaining her decision to run away (Act I, Scene i)

b)   a video diary of one of the lovers, trying to account for the quarrels and changes of heart (Act III, Scene ii)

c)   an interview with Bottom on the success of his performance as Pyramus (Act IV, Scene i)

Themes

Love and marriage Ask your students to consider what Shakespeare tells us about love and marriage in this play. Did he think you should only marry for love? Did he sympathize most with Hermia or Helena? What did he mean by these quotations?

Act I, Scene i, line 134   (The course of true love never did run smooth)

Act I, Scene i, line 234   (Love looks not with the eyes, but with the mind)

They might explore their ideas by writing an interview with Shakespeare, in which they focus upon his attitudes to love and marriage.

Obedience At the end of the play, Hermia ends up marrying Lysander, but was she right to disobey her father at the start? Titania does not comply with Oberon's wishes and is punished. Encourage your students to discuss how they feel about these situations and whether this play gives us a glimpse of what life was like for women in Elizabethan times. These statements might be a starting point.

● It's not real life, just a story to entertain.
● Shakespeare disagreed with how the women were treated.
● Shakespeare couldn't show Titania to be more powerful than the male Oberon.

Magical influence In this play, Shakespeare creates a world where mishaps, such as losing your way or falling from a stool, are actually caused by the mischievous Puck. Ask your students to think of other accidents or errors that could put down to Puck, e.g. computer errors and lost homework.

Shakespeare's Language

Magical verse As in other plays such as *The Tempest* and *Macbeth*, Shakespeare uses a different format of verse for magical characters. It consists of shorter, more rhythmical lines and the content tends to refer to the natural world of plants and creatures. Direct your students to analyse some of the fairy verse, e.g. the song in Act 2, Scene 2. Then ask them to create their own fairy verse, perhaps based on one of the following:

- the further adventures of the mischievous Puck
- Titania's strange 'dream'
- a song in praise of Oberon and Titania.

The language of love This play abounds with words of love, e.g. 'beauteous Hermia', 'sweet lady', 'I swear to thee by Cupid's strongest bow'. Some of them are overblown and exaggerated for comic effect, e.g. 'O Helen, goddess, nymph, perfect, divine'. The students can make a study of this language, noting features such as comparisons, classical references, vows, etc. Ask them to use this knowledge to create a love letter from one of the characters to another.

Insults As well as words of affection, there are also a host of insults hurled around, e.g. 'thou burr', 'canker-blossom', 'puppet'. Challenge your students to find as many of them as they can in order to compile a dictionary of insults. They might like to try them out on each other.

Exploring with Drama

Book the hall or push back the desks because the best way to study a great play is through drama. Students of all ages will benefit from a dramatic encounter with *A Midsummer Night's Dream*. They will enjoy the opportunity to act out a scene or two, or to explore the situations through improvisation, e.g. by putting a character in the 'hot seat' for questioning by others.

Tableaux Ask your students to create a tableau or freeze-frame of the first scene in the play, showing the Duke, Hippolyta, Egeus, and the four lovers. The positions of the characters should say something about their relationships and status within the scene/play. Bring the tableaux to life briefly by having each character say something in character. Next, create a tableau for the last scene, with the same characters. Again, the tableau may be brought to life briefly. There should be a clear contrast between both scenes.

The lost lovers This activity looks at Act 3, Scene 2 in which the lovers are led astray in the forest by Puck and eventually fall asleep. Choose four students to be the lovers and one to be Puck. The rest of the class will fill the available space and become trees! As each lover enters the forest, one-by-one, led on by the invisible Puck, the enchanted trees come to life, confusing the route through the forest. The trees are firmly rooted and so students cannot move their feet, but they can move their 'branches' as long as they do not touch anyone. As they grow tired, each lover lies down to rest. They should be encouraged to refine their performance, considering how movement and sound can be used most effectively.

A reduced version Test the students' understanding of the plot by asking groups to create a reduced version of the whole play. They will first need to decide on the key events and the essential characters, and they should try to include some quotations in their version.

Writing about *A Midsummer Night's Dream*

If your students have to write about *A Midsummer Night's Dream* for coursework or for examinations, you may wish to give them this general guidance.

- Read the question or task carefully, highlight the key words, and answer all parts of the question.
- Planning is essential. Plan what will be in each paragraph. You can change your plan if necessary.
- Avoid retelling the story.
- *A Midsummer Night's Dream* is a play, so consider the impact or effect on the audience.

- Use the Point, Evidence, Explanation (PEE) structure to explain points.
- Adding Evaluation (PEEE!) will gain you higher marks.
- Keep quotations short.
- Avoid referring to a film version of the play, unless this is part of your task.

Further Reading and Resources

General

Fantasia, Louis, *Instant Shakespeare: a practical guide for actors, directors and teachers* (A & C Black, 2002)

Greer, Germaine, *Shakespeare: a very short introduction* (Oxford, 2002)

Hall, Peter, *Shakespeare's Advice to the Players* (Oberon Books, 2003)

Holden, Anthony, *Shakespeare: his life and work* (Abacus, 2002)

Kneen, Judith, *Teaching Shakespeare from Transition to Test* (Oxford University Press, 2004)

McConnell, Louise, *Exit, Pursued by a Bear – Shakespeare's characters, plays, poems, history and stagecraft* (Bloomsbury, 2003)

McLeish and Unwin, *A Pocket Guide to Shakespeare's Plays* (Faber and Faber, 1998)

Muirden, James, *Shakespeare in a Nutshell: A Rhyming Guide to All the Plays* (Constable, 2004)

Wood, Michael, *In Search of Shakespeare* (BBC, 2003)

Children's/students' books

Carpenter, Humphrey, *Shakespeare Without the Boring Bits* (Viking, 1994)

Deary, Terry, *Top Ten Shakespeare Stories* (Scholastic, 1998)

Ganeri, Anita, *What they don't tell you about Shakespeare* (Hodder, 1996)

Garfield, Leon, *Shakespeare Stories* (Puffin, 1997)

Garfield, Leon, *Shakespeare: The Animated Tales* (Egmont, 2002)

Lamb, Charles and Mary, *Tales from Shakespeare* (Puffin, 1987)

McCaughrean, Geraldine, *Stories from Shakespeare* (Orion, 1997)

Williams, Marcia, *Mr William Shakespeare's Plays* (Walker, 2000)

Websites

The Complete Works of Shakespeare
http://the-tech.mit.edu/Shakespeare/

Elizabethan pronunciation
Includes information on insults.
http://www.renfaire.com/Language/index.html

Encyclopaedia Britannica – Shakespeare and the Globe: Then and Now
Information about the Globe and the theatre in Shakespeare's times.
http://search.eb.com/shakespeare/index2.html

The Royal Shakespeare Company website
As well as information on the theatre company, there are resources
on the plays and the life and times of Shakespeare.
http://www.rsc.org.uk/home/index.asp

The Shakespeare Birthplace Trust
Information on his works, life, and times.
http://www.shakespeare.org.uk/homepage

Shakespeare's Globe
Information on the Globe Theatre, London.
http://www.shakespeares-globe.org/

Shakespeare Illustrated
An excellent source of paintings and pictures based on
Shakespeare's plays.
http://www.emory.edu/ENGLISH/classes/Shakespeare_Illustrated/
Shakespeare.html

Spark Notes: A Midsummer Night's Dream
An online study guide.
http://www.sparknotes.com/shakespeare/msnd/

Mr William Shakespeare and the Internet
A comprehensive guide to Shakespeare resources on the Internet.
http://shakespeare.palomar.edu/

Film, video, DVD, and audio

A Midsummer Night's Dream
Directed by Michael Hoffman (1998)

A Midsummer Night's Dream
Directed by Adrian Noble (1996)

Shakespeare: *A Midsummer Night's Dream* (audio CD)
BBC Radio Collection (1999)